To the Gemperle's

God bless you!

NO PRICE TOO HIGH

NO PRICE TOO HIGH

A Pentecostal Preacher
Becomes Catholic

The Inspirational Story of
ALEX JONES

as told to
Diane Marie Morey Hanson

and with a special section
THE CONVERSION STORY OF
DONNA JONES

IGNATIUS PRESS   SAN FRANCISCO

Cover photograph of Alex Jones by Diane M. Hanson
Cover design by Roxanne Mei Lum

© 2006 Ignatius Press, San Francisco
All rights reserved
ISBN 978-0-89870-919-3
ISBN 0-89870-919-9
Library of Congress Control Number 2005933378
Printed in the United States of America ∞

DEDICATIONS

To Dennis Walters, Ph.D., a friend who gave two years of his life helping Donna and me to understand the teachings of the Roman Catholic Church. And to the fifty-four people that sought truth for themselves and came with us into the Church.

— Alex Jones

To my husband Alex, who desired truth above friends, family, and material possessions. To our sons, their wives, and their families, who followed the Spirit of Christ through my husband into the Church. To Bernice, Dianne, and Debbie, for their love. To the brothers and sisters who prayed for us and supported us as we made our transition into Christ's Church. And last, but not least, to the fifty-two who came with us and endured ridicule by their peers and families. They trusted, through Alex, God's promise for their lives.

— Donna Jones

To my husband Bart and my children, Lora, Eric, Lisa, Jeff, Scott, and Leah, for their incredible support and sharing of my time as I worked on this book. To my good friend Steve Ray for his encouragement, enthusiasm, advice, time, and, along with his wonderful wife, Janet, for doing the first proofing of the completed manuscript. And most of all, to the guidance of the Holy Spirit.

— Diane Hanson

THE PEARLS

A father gave his little daughter a lovely string of imitation pearls. The little girl was thrilled with the gift and wore the prized necklace every day. Even as a teenager, she treasured her special gift.

When she had grown into a beautiful young woman, the father asked his daughter to give the necklace back to him. She was dismayed and at first protested. But the father insisted, gently repeating the words, "Trust me!" Reluctantly, but with faith in her father, she returned the necklace.

As soon as he had taken the childhood gift away, he extended his other hand, which held a new black velvet box. With a smile of pure joy, he handed it to his daughter. Her eyes widened with surprise and awe as she opened the box and gazed upon the most stunning string of real pearls she had ever seen. She quickly realized that what she had before was very beautiful and very good, but paled in comparison to the real thing.

CONTENTS

FOREWORD

I will never forget the phone call that evening. The unfamiliar voice on the other end of the line said, "You don't know me, but my name is Alex Jones. Of all the men in all the world I need to talk to you."

I was a bit surprised and hesitatingly said, "All right, what can I do for you?"

Alex said, "You converted from Evangelical Protestantism to the Catholic Church, right?"

I said, "Yes I did."

Then Alex quickly responded, "You are the only one I know of who has done that—so you will understand what I am going through. Can we talk?"

A few days later we met at a Big Boy Restaurant in Detroit. We had a delightful time, and I knew I had discovered a kindred spirit. I was impressed with Alex Jones the first time I laid eyes on him. He had a seriousness about him, but his soberness did not overshadow his sense of adventure and curiosity. I could see the intensity in his eyes, and as we began to talk I saw in him a rare honesty and depth. This was not a frivolous man. It was obvious that he had latched on to something and was not going to let it go.

It was the first of many lunches at Big Boy. We talked for almost three hours. I recounted my own conversion to the Catholic Church as I answered his rapid-fire questions. And they were not your average questions. Alex is a thinker, and he was thinking deeply. I still remember his eyes. They seemed to be dancing with the wonderment of a child, yet with the passion for truth of a sage. He was visibly excited, yet cautious and prudent. He wanted to know, but he was not reckless. He knew the Bible well and wanted everything to line up with the written Word of God. His eyes would darken and his eyebrows furl as he wrestled with new angles on the truth as they conflicted with old religious prejudices. I was watching a transformation take place right before my eyes.

The Lord had pulled back the curtain, and Alex had caught a glimpse of the early Church, and that short vision had set him on a quest. This quest was a dangerous thing for Alex to pursue since it could turn his life upside down and bring to a screeching halt the pastor's life he knew and loved. I warned him several times. "Alex," I said, "I want you to understand the full import of the questions you are asking, and the doors you are opening. It is the most exciting adventure you will ever embark upon, but at the same time, Alex, it can bring great pain and suffering. You stand to gain much, but you also could lose your family, your friends, your livelihood, and the Maranatha Church, which you have pastored all these years. You are at a fork in the road, Alex; move slowly and prayerfully."

We talked on the phone many times and continued our monthly lunches together. He was always bright-eyed and full of questions. After the first few meetings, I knew he had gone too far ever to turn back. He had discovered the Catholic Church, the best-kept secret in the world, and like the parable Jesus told of the priceless pearl, Alex was willing to give up everything to own the treasure for himself. No price was too high for Alex once he glimpsed the eternal treasure.

A short time later, Alex invited my wife, Janet, and me to his home to meet his beautiful and intelligent wife, Donna.

We were soon to find she also had a deep spirituality. She walked with Jesus as few people do, and she talked and lived as though she and Jesus were close friends. She was also, we discovered, not too fond of the Catholic Church or the direction her husband was taking. We tried to listen and share without pushing. Donna also had the eyes and manners of a person deeply concerned about truth and willing to take a stand for truth no matter what it cost her. And at this point she thought that truth was against the Catholic Church. But we loved her passion for truth and knew that if she continued to oppose the Church with *honest* questions, she would eventually see the fullness of the faith, and the Bible would open to her as never before.

My wife, Janet, took a liking to Donna. She prayed for her every day and kept in close contact. Had my wife been pushy with Donna it might have been the perfect excuse for Donna to bolt and run, but Janet was calm and patient. She knew that Donna was honest and that the truth would eventually dawn on Donna, and she wanted to be there to guide and coach her along the way.

I will never forget one day when I was reading my e-mails: I called Janet to come quickly. With smiles of joy and tears in our eyes, we read the words from Alex: "Donna wants me to tell you she is Catholic." Donna probably expected that we wouldn't believe it, but we did. Even though her conversion had taken a different course and time frame than Alex', we had seen the transformation coming. In conversations, we had seen the same "dangerous" wonderment and curiosity in her eyes—at least dangerous for one who wanted to withstand the Catholic Church. We had known it was just a matter of time. We rejoiced at the words we read in that e-mail. Janet called Donna to congratulate her.

The rest is a matter of history and is well told in the two stories you are about to read in this book. The reader is fortunate to have two heartfelt stories in one. They are very different stories, yet they dovetail so beautifully. God is a master craftsman, and you will see his skill as he worked in this family, knitting two souls together as they traversed the dangerous and unknown paths. God shone his light on their paths, not far into the future, but only the light they needed for each step. Even if God *had* given them a glimpse of their lives together as Catholics now, they wouldn't have believed it.

We were very emotional at the Easter Vigil of 2001. A significant number of members of an African-American Pentecostal congregation—fifty-four persons in all (including two who entered later on Easter Sunday)—being received into the Catholic Church was not an everyday occurrence. Janet was Donna's sponsor, and I kept my camera flashing. It was joyful and moving. We had grown to love Alex and Donna dearly. To see them enraptured before the altar brought tears to our eyes and the eyes of many others. This was the end of a long journey for them. It had been a journey fraught with pain, loss, suffering, and betrayal. But it had also been a frolicking adventure filled with excitement, the joy of discovery, the making of new friends, and joining in the sumptuous feast of the Church. The journey had been bittersweet. But now on that eventful evening, one journey ended and another began.

Looking back on the whole process, we again marvel at the hand of God working in two wonderful souls. We are filled with joy at the blessings God has poured on them and their family since they set their faces like flint to follow God's lead no matter what the cost. We also marvel in the great blessing these two have been to the Church worldwide. They are opening doors for many folks who would have never been open to the fullness of the faith in the Catholic Church. With great pleasure, I watch as Alex preaches to large crowds who are deeply moved by his story and wisdom. I join them as they laugh and cry and are moved to deeper commitment and love for our Lord Jesus Christ.

You are about to embark on a great journey. You are about to share their joys and sorrows. Alex and Donna have opened their souls to us and have invited us to share their intellectual, personal, cultural, religious, emotional, and theological struggles. You will be blessed and encouraged. You will be challenged and edified. You will thank God for this brother and sister in the Lord.

Steve Ray
Author of *Crossing the Tiber*
August 8, 2005

PART ONE

ALEX' STORY

I

Homecoming

This was it.

Finally, after three years of agonizing personal pain, I was holding the Real Thing right there in my hands. This was my Lord and my God.

I had first found him as a Pentecostal in 1958, at the age of sixteen, through a most powerful spiritual experience. Pentecostals and charismatics call it the "baptism in the Holy Spirit". In that amazing encounter, the resurrected Christ tenderly held me in his hands. Now, more than forty years later, I was gently holding him in mine.

And so there on my knees, I slowly and carefully brought the Bread of Life to my mouth, the True Manna, the Flesh of Christ, who so willingly gave his Flesh for the life of the world. As I took him into myself, I was overcome with both awe and joy.

My First Holy Communion—I will never forget that—that feeling that I had finally come the closest I could ever get to Christ in this life. Even to this very day, when the Body of our Lord is placed in my hand, I look at him with wonderment and awe, that he would actually give himself to me—offer himself to me as food. What incomprehensible humility!

Receiving Communion is no longer just a part of worship for me; now I see that this is my God who humbles himself to meet me in love and forgiveness. The Victim of

Calvary, who takes away the sins of the world, actually offers himself as food and drink to me—a sinner—that I might eat and be nourished with life eternal.

I get very emotional every time I think about it. It is the realization of the spiritual impact—that this is not just common bread and common wine—this is the Flesh of our Lord and the Blood of our Lord. For this alone I was willing to walk away from everything I had worked for and held dear. I walked away from friends, family, ministry, leadership, livelihood—everything!

I had to do it. There was nothing else for me to do. How could I deny what I had come to know to be true? How could I look into the face of Truth and say, "That's nice history, but it will cause me problems"?

So I said Yes to God, and that Yes has cost me dearly.

You see, until 1998, I had never even entertained what would then have been the utterly ridiculous idea of becoming Catholic! I was happy as a Pentecostal Evangelical pastor and wanted nothing more than to finish my tenure as a pastor, pass on my work to a qualified minister, and retire to teaching or some other laudable work.

I had grown up with the understanding that Catholics were the most wicked people on the face of the earth. They were not even Christians. The Catholic Church was the great whore of Babylon, as revealed in Revelation 17. And the pope—with his tiara surrounded with Latin words that, when put into their numeric values, came out to 666—was the absolute beast.

While my views moderated considerably over the years, my entrance into the Catholic Church was still nothing short of a miraculous event—from my unquenchable desire for knowledge and truth to the people God placed along the pathway of my journey.

When I recognized that the Catholic Church was *the* Church of Jesus Christ as it has always been from the beginning—unchangeable, full of glory—I had to be a part of it. Knowing that this was his Church and that this was Christianity in its ultimate form—I could not in good conscience say that I love Jesus and remain out of the Church for the sake of pride, convenience, or money. For it had sunk in to me that the Catholic Church was *the* Church.

And so, for me, coming into the Catholic Church was such a joy and relief. I felt like a sojourner, like a wanderer who had finally—by Providence—found a way home. Nearly sixty years of formation—trials, tribulations, triumphs, successes and failures, joys and sorrows—had culminated in my attaining the "fullness" of Christian faith and life. The night of the Easter Vigil, April 14, 2001, at Saint Suzanne's Catholic Church in Detroit, I felt relieved that I had finally traversed those difficult roads of discovery, of rejection, of uncertainty, of not knowing what would happen to me, or who would come with me.

There were fifty-one members of my congregation who did come with me that night including my wife, Donna; our three sons, Joseph, Benjamin, and Marc; all three daughters-in-law, Bianca, Tamala, and Caleetha; five grandchildren; my sister Gwen; my niece Linda; my great-nephew Lonnie; and my great-niece Lindsey. Two others joined the Church the next day, making a total of fifty-four.

On that cool April evening in 2001, I had the distinct feeling of being among an even larger family. It was a feeling that only one who has been away from home for a long time and who has come back to the family can feel. I was *home*!

I still feel that to this very day. I'm home! I'm where I'm supposed to be. The uncertainty, the wandering, the searching, the feeling of something missing; all of that has disappeared. This is it. This is home. I recognize this as the Big House. I was born in a comfortable tent filled with joy and love, but it was just a tent in the backyard of the Big House. Now I'm *in* the Big House. I'm *home!*

It's been five years now since I've become Catholic, and I look back and marvel at this bittersweet experience. The greatest bitterness is the loss of some of my friends and parishioners. These are godly people, holy people, but they could not comprehend what I had come to understand with great clarity. I mourn the loss of their fellowship, and, even though they still love me, I realize that our relationship can never be the same again.

The sweetness, which far outweighs the bitterness, is continually learning more about the faith that Christ has preserved within the Catholic Church. The knowledge is amazing. It is as though coming out of a five-by-five dark closet into a courtyard blazing with noonday light. It is as though shackles have been taken off of my mind. I can use my intellect without the fear of losing my spirituality or heavenly focus.

To be exposed to the teachings of the Church, enriched by two thousand years of saints, scholars, and theologians, is overwhelming. There is so much that I could never possibly absorb it all in my lifetime—the writings of the Church Fathers, the teachings of the Church, the sacraments, the saints, Mary.

And what a joy it is to discover that the Kingdom of God is to be enjoyed not only by its inhabitants, but the main goal is to take that Kingdom into our world and transform the face of the earth by the life of the Kingdom. As our Lord said in Matthew 25, we are to take care of those who are incarcerated, to demonstrate life and mercy. Living the Gospel is so rich. How fully I now understand that the core of the Gospel is ministry—not the ministry of preaching and teaching—but the ministry of serving others. It is putting others before yourself. That is an important result of the Gospel message.

This is the Church, this is the society, and these are the people of God. The Catholic Church is the original Pentecostal Church. Think about it! It is the Church of the apostles and their successors. This is the hierarchy that Jesus left. This is the foundation he established. This is the authority he gave. And to be a part of that Kingdom means more than anything in the world to me.

If I had never learned about the great doctors of the Church, if I had never learned about theology and philosophy, just to know that I'm in the Church of the Upper Room, my Lord's Church, is more than sufficient. Everything else is just icing on the cake.

To this day I am in awe of how God led me into his Church. It has been an amazing process. This journey has been and continues to be nothing short of phenomenal—and it is just the beginning!

2

Oh, What a Life!

I had a very, *very* good childhood. In fact, it was absolutely great! I remember just loving life. I didn't have any hang-ups as a young child. I have warm memories of those days—walking down the street in the summertime—just clacking my stick across the picket fence, looking up at the blue sky and arriving home to a good hot dinner.

Life was great in my eyes for a number of reasons. I had a mother who stayed home and took care of us and made sure we all ate dinner together. We all sat down at the table together every night, and we talked together. We were *family*—my mom, Margaret, my dad, Alex, my sister, Gwen—four years older than I was, my brother, Harold—eight years older than I, and me. I was the baby of the family.

I was born in Detroit, Michigan, on a Friday, September 19, 1941. It was a difficult pregnancy for my mother, and the doctors had wanted her to abort me. But she refused the abortion and stayed in bed for months just to give me life.

She has been a woman of prayer all her life, and she raised me in her church, which I absolutely loved in my early years. I cherished those days as a member of Zion Congregational Church of God in Christ on Mack Avenue in Detroit, and I was ready to be baptized at the age of nine. I loved it. I just *loved* church!

Church was a very significant part of my mother's life, but not my dad's. I never saw my dad in church during my youth. He never went to church. He had been hurt as a young man. His first wife had received some bad advice in her church, and it had cost her life. I guess he just couldn't forgive the church because he believed the people there robbed him of the woman he loved, so for a long time after that he did not go to church.

But my dad was a very good man with good Christian values—even though without formal religion. He was very family oriented, loved his kids and wife, and worked hard every day. His routine was to get up at four in the morning; take the 5 A.M. bus to the Revere Copper and Brass factory on West Jefferson every weekday; take the bus home at the end of the workday; get home; drink a jumbo beer (we call it a forty-ounce now); read the sports section; fall asleep; wake up to eat dinner; watch television; take a bath; and go to bed.

That was his life. He never really wanted to go anywhere. He just loved his family and loved staying home. That's another reason my childhood was so great—we knew we were loved. I think about it now, and I have very warm feelings of a good stable home and a dad and mother who really loved me. Life was just great!

I loved my dad so much when I was a kid that I used to see him as someone who could do anything. My dad had a broad back, and I had seen him carry an icebox upstairs on his back. I thought he could fix anything, and I thought he could do anything. And I loved the smell of his pipe tobacco. I loved to go for rides with him in the Model T Ford. He had to crank it up to get it started, and I loved to ride up on the front seat with him, just putt-putting along and drinking in the aroma of his pipe tobacco.

My dad was a good-looking man. He was White for all practical purposes. His father, Joseph Jones, was a White landowner in Enterprise, Mississippi, and his mother was a very light mulatto. My grandfather really loved my grandmother, but because of the racial laws in Mississippi at that time, he could never marry her. The races were not allowed to mix back then. They couldn't even live together, but they must have found ways to *get* together because they had nine or ten kids, and my dad, born in 1898, was the only boy.

All my dad's sisters had White features with blue eyes, and my dad's eyes were hazel. He had straight hair, and he could easily pass as a White man. In fact, people always thought he was White.

He liked to tell us the story about the time the White lady got on the bus he was riding to work. She boarded the bus and asked my dad, "Mister, can I sit next to you?"

He answered, "Sure, if you want to."

As she sat down next to him she confided, "I just don't want to sit next to no niggers!"

Now you have to keep in mind that this was in the 1940s. My dad thought it was hilarious, but was able to keep a straight face when he answered her, "Well that's okay; you can sit next to me."

Early in his life he had decided to identify with Black people and to live what he really felt he was. His decision was cemented when he witnessed a lynching after leaving home at the age of fifteen. He traveled to Saint Louis where he saw White men dragging a Black man chained to the back of their car through the streets. They unhooked him from the car, burned him to a crisp, and threw the charred body over a pier.

That was something my dad could never, ever forget. He talked about it all the time, and you could tell that, even after so many years, it really, really hurt him. That event not only made him determined to identify with Black people, but it also caused him to develop a distinct dislike for White folks.

When my mom and dad met, Dad had a drinking problem, and he had the wisdom to see that being married to my mom would bring a new quality to his life. She literally saved his life, convincing him to tone down his drinking mostly to just one day a week, with only one beer on the other days.

Still, his drinking grieved her because she was a holy woman. I never heard my mother use an inappropriate word. She would never even say "butt" or "bootie". To her that was sinful. When my dad got drunk, he would throw out some pretty salty language, and you could see how upset that made my mom.

But Dad had a tremendous sense of humor and a sharp wit. He would crack jokes and was the life of the family. Since he didn't take religion seriously, he had funny nicknames for everyone at the church. He had tons of preacher jokes too. He kept us all laughing—except Ma.

I must have gotten my sense of humor from my father, because my mother had absolutely no sense of humor at all. None. It was all business with her, and it was all Jesus. She prayed all the time. She prayed night and day, and God did wonderful things for my mother. She had some tremendous religious experiences.

Ma was the disciplinarian in our home. Dad just worked hard and loved us. If Dad said, "I'll give you a 'whoopin'", we would go, "Yeah, right!" and then burst out laughing.

Not so with my mother! She would say, "Go out in the backyard and cut me a switch."

I would plead with her, "Oh, come on, Ma, I'm sorry!"

"No. Just go cut me a switch", she would reply. So I would go out and try to get the smallest one that would break easily. Ma would just say, "Okay, I see I have to go and get one myself." She would go get a long one with the pliable fronds that wouldn't break but would wrap around you.

Then she'd start whipping us, and we'd start crying, and she'd say, "Just shut up that noise!"

So we'd stop crying, and she'd say, "Oh, so you ain't going to cry, huh?" I probably got the switch the most, and I probably deserved it.

At an early age I found out that my mother's best friends were her sisters and brothers. When my relatives came over, they would sit and talk about the Bible, about the Rapture, and about the goodness of the Lord. When I was a little kid, I would just hang around and listen to them. It put within me a desire to really be like them. I would listen to those conversations, and I would yearn to be like those good people. I always felt they were different.

Even as a youngster, I really wanted to know God. One of the most significant events in my young life was my baptism at the age of nine. We knew nothing about the baptism of regeneration, but I knew baptism was significant, that now I was a Christian, now I was part of God's people. I felt that, and knew now that demands were placed on me by God.

But as I moved into my teen years, I grew more and more rebellious, and I grew to dislike the father I had idolized. I thought he wasn't a real man. Once a week, on Thursdays when he got paid, he got lit up. He would drink a lot of gin, and sometimes he would say things that would embarrass me. He was an emotional kind of guy, and I sometimes saw him cry. He loved country music, and even that made him cry. I didn't feel that real men cried or said they were sorry. Real men were strong and forceful. I had this distorted image of what manhood was, and Dad just didn't fit that image, so I grew to despise him.

Also I began to grow away from the church. Even though I had a great pastor, I was developing into a teenager, and I wanted to do what my friends did—and that wasn't church related. I began smoking when I was about twelve, and started to drink a lot by the time I was fourteen or fifteen. I didn't do drugs, but I did a lot of other untellables. I look back on it now, and it wasn't all that bad. We didn't hurt anybody, but we'd get mind-bending drunk, and we'd do some pretty dumb things.

The older I got, the further I moved away from church. I began to despise church. It was boring, and to me it seemed that no one was there except old people—just checking in before they checked out! It was *so* borrrrrring! I wanted to live—LIVE! I wanted to party, and I figured, when I got older—like around thirty-nine—I would consider going back to church.

So, by my teen years, my mother began having a problem with getting me to church. I resented being told to go to church, but that didn't seem to faze her. She didn't swear or even raise her voice. She would simply say, "In twenty minutes, you be ready."

Well, I would take that Bible and throw it around, and I'd curse it. "I hate this", I would yell. Twenty minutes later, I was always ready to go.

I remember riding to church with Mom, and she would be singing songs; in the summertime the windows were rolled down, and everyone could hear her: "The Lord lifted me!"

I would scoot way down in my seat, so my friends wouldn't see me as we pulled up to a stoplight. I'd plead with her, "Mom, do you *have* to sing?" She would just ignore me and keep right on singing.

Looking back now, those were good days in the church, and the people there really were very good people. It was just that I hated being there. And I would get some of the worst slaps in the world at church. I would sit next to my mother and make some noise or do something dumb and POW! I'd sit up straight.

On one occasion, I asked my mother if I could go to the lavatory during the service. She granted permission but warned me to be back in a few minutes. I went downstairs, and I had a comic book with me. As I began to read, I kind of forgot about the few-minute warning. I was engrossed in my comic book when I heard footsteps coming my way, but I was too dumb to look up. POW! I saw stars and heard my mom's voice, "Didn't I tell you only a few minutes?"

And so, by the time I was a teenager, I hated church. I thought my mom was the meanest woman on the face of the earth. I thought religion was for old folks, and all I wanted was to have a good-time party. Man, I loved life! I hated school and church, but how I loved life! Then, when I turned fifteen, I got my driver's permit and had the opportunity to drive. The problem was we only had one car, and it was my mom's car. My dad didn't even drive it to work. He took the bus. So you only drove that car where that car went, and that car only went to church. If I wanted to drive, I had to drive to church, but once I got there I was just biding my time until I could drive back home again.

Then along came the two-week revival at our church. I was a junior at Pershing High School in Detroit at that time. My mother kept talking about some lady named Mother Boyd being there, and I thought, yeah, right, she was probably some old woman that drooled and walked with a shuffle and wore a dress down to her ankles. But I went to the revival anyway because, you know, I had a chance to drive.

And I was just sitting there when Mother Estella Boyd walked in, and she just blew me away. She was probably in her mid-thirties—a *fine*-looking woman—not exactly what I expected her to look like, certainly not like the church mothers I had seen! She was really beautiful! And talk about spiritual power—I thought, oh man, this is very interesting! She was a very powerful, powerful evangelist.

So while I was there I thought I might just as well take in the sights—I didn't want to be a part of it—just kind of take a look. I stood and watched those gathered and wondered: What in the world is going on here? And I saw something I had never seen before. Some of the young people that I knew—and we had done some things together that we shouldn't have—were praying! They were receiving the baptism of the Holy Spirit. They were full of the Holy Spirit. And I knew it had to be real, because these guys wouldn't fake it. We hated church! Man, we'd sneak around the corner and buy cigarettes and smoke them while the preacher was preaching.

Now here they were praying to God with their hands raised and tears streaming down their faces. That really intrigued me. So I came back on the following evenings—not just to drive—but to see what was going on. Young people draw young people, and these were young singles and married couples. I'd never seen anything like this in church before. I knew I was looking at miracles. This was awesome!

To make matters even more intriguing, I began to notice that when I attended this revival, I felt good. And the more I came to church, the cleaner I felt. This was great, I thought, but I still had no intention to *like* church. In fact, I went out that Saturday night with the boys. We picked up our girlfriends, and they all said, "Hey man, Jones is trying to get religion!"

Well, I called them every name in the book! I had to prove to them that that wasn't true. I called them everything I could think of. I talked about their mothers *and* their fathers. I got profane. I had to prove I was still the same tough guy and that I certainly *wasn't* seeking religion!

But they were right. I just didn't want to admit it.

The two weeks passed by quickly, and I continued to feel drawn to that revival. I had started going because of the driving, but within a few days I was going because it felt good to be there.

Then came the day I will never forget—it was August 23, 1958, about 10:30 on a Saturday evening. The revival was over, and there was a convocation of about ten or fifteen churches that had come together for reading and to hear a preacher from Chicago. There was no air conditioning, and it was incredibly hot in the church. I remember the preacher's sermon was "As an Eagle Stirs Her Nest". But what he said about an eagle and her nest, I have no idea. It's gone because what happened afterward was so powerful that it erased just about everything else that happened before.

I do remember that when he finished preaching, the three or four hundred gathered there that night broke into song. They all stood to sing—it was a loud Pentecostal song— and they were getting into it, just clapping and rocking and having a good time and enjoying themselves. I had my new charcoal gray suit on, and I felt pretty good too, but, you know, I was still Alex.

My cousin Leroy, who was about fourteen years older, was sitting next to me. He was a U.S. Marine and had just come home from Korea. He had been at the Chosen Reservoir in Northern Korea and had survived the Chinese onslaught there. He was a big guy, about six-two, six-three, and he was strong. I admired and had great respect for him. He was my idea of a man. He was my hero.

So when he said, "Stand up and praise the Lord", I stood up and clapped my hands slightly.

He said, "Tell God, 'thank you'."

Well, my sister had told me to do that too, but I had told her to bug off. I wasn't about to tell my cousin to bug off though. So I said, "Thank you, Jesus."

And he said, "Tell him again."

So I said a little louder, "Thank you, Jesus."

He said, "Tell him again!"

So I raised my voice and shouted, "*Thank you, Jesus!*"

After that third time—it was all over.

I was standing there clapping, and it seemed as though time stopped. It was as though I was just enveloped by a tremendous presence, and that presence I knew was God. I was enfolded by a presence that was indescribable, and for the first time in my life, I knew God was real. That was the very first thought that came into my mind: "God does really live. He really does exist."

I forgot about my cousin. I forgot about the music, the church, time, and space. I forgot about *everything*. I was transfixed with this presence—a most powerful presence, a warmth—almost like a heat, yet it was not a physical heat. It was something I could sense. It was real, and it had a loving warmth.

And then it dawned on me, for the first time in my life, that I was a sinner! I was stunned that God would reveal himself to me, and that he would let his presence be known to me, and I was totally unworthy of that. I began to cry and to ask for his forgiveness and for him to wash me clean. I will never forget that; I began to plead, "Please forgive me!" Even though all this took place almost fifty years ago, I still get teary eyed when I recall that night.

There was an incredible dialogue going on between me and God. I really didn't know what I was saying because I had no knowledge of theology, but I felt I needed to be washed. The words would come to me, and I would repeat them over and over, for I don't know how long: "Save me. Forgive me. Wash me. Make me whole."

By this time I had collapsed into a heap on the floor, although it didn't seem like it. I remember falling down, but it was insignificant. Normally, if I were to fall down on the floor in front of people, I would be embarrassed. But it meant nothing to me then because I was in the presence of God. My sister later told me that by that time everyone in the church had stopped because they realized something was going on, and they were getting excited. They knew me. I had a reputation for not being a religious person, and they knew I didn't like church.

My pastor, who was eighty-four years old at the time, came down from the pulpit while I was lying on the floor and put his hand on my chest and began praying for me, asking God to fill my life and my heart. And then that joy and that peace you can only experience—you cannot describe—began to flow through my heart and my life. I was no longer myself in any way, and this language was just flowing out of me. I remember trying to say something, but it wasn't coming out in English. This was all new to me, and I didn't know what was going on.

I reached up and grabbed my pastor's arm and pulled myself up, and when I opened my eyes, the whole church seemed aglow. It was luminous. And I began to preach. I had no fear of people, and it was just flowing out of me. It just wasn't me because I was such an introvert around people. I was not even seventeen yet, and I was saying, "The Lord will return. He *will* come back again. He *will* come back."

By this time the church was in bedlam. To the people there it was a miracle.

Then, before I went back to my seat, I made the sign of the cross in the air like a priest makes a blessing. And I wondered, why did I do that? Now I know; that was the symbol of absolution; I felt forgiven.

After that, I was literally drunk—just like when you drink too much alcohol and become inebriated. I was drunk—only I was drunk in the Spirit. Someone had to hold onto me. By this time the service had been dismissed, and people were bringing their little children up to me to pray for them. Here I was, just three feet from the streets, and now people were bringing their children to me for blessings. I would lay hands on them and pray for them, and all the while this language was just pouring out of my heart.

That continued all the way home. I just couldn't stop. All the way home I was praising God—I was enraptured. My dad was in bed when I got home, and when he heard all the noise he came downstairs and asked, "What's going on?"

When I saw him, for the first time since I was a little child, I loved him. All of the anger, all of the bitterness, all of the hurt was *gone*! And I said, "Dad, I love you."

That night I slept on a cot downstairs. The next day my dad told me that he came down during the night just to look at me and try to figure out what was going on. "You were still doing that thing—speaking in that heavenly language—even while you were sleeping", he said. "I just stood there and watched you, and it just poured out of you."

When I woke up that next day, *I felt good!* I knew I had met God, and now I was redeemed. My friend Roland came by that morning and blew his horn. He was my number one buddy. We cruised together, we dated girls together, we did everything together, and we were supposed to go cruising that Sunday. I was so excited I ran out to meet him.

I said, "Roland, man, I got saved last night. I found the Lord!" I thought, of all my friends, he would be the happiest for me—I had found the Lord, and it was a miraculous thing. I thought everyone would enjoy my exuberance and share my joy. I was wrong.

Roland was smoking a cigarette, and he just looked at me, flipped the ashes off, and said, "Man, I don't want to hear that." It came as a shock to me.

I said, "Okay. I've got to go." Then I ran back into the house, and I didn't see him again for forty years. He went his way, and I went mine.

So for me, the group that I had run with ceased to exist. It was no loss. A whole new world had opened to me that I hadn't known existed; another aspect of being. I had to understand it, and I wanted to know this God who loved me. I wanted to know his purpose and plan.

What had happened to me was awesome. It was a conversion that proved to be the starting point of my quest for truth and my quest to know God. So nothing else mattered. It may have been a little extreme, but I had no desire for television, no desire for movies, and no desire for material things. I wanted to understand what had happened to me and who this was who had called me into his grace.

I took my Pall Mall cigarettes and threw them away. When I returned the books I had stolen two years earlier to the school library, the librarian looked at me as though I were nuts. But I had to make straight paths for my feet because I knew that the God who had called me demanded holiness. To live in fellowship with him, I had to do what I did. Anything that I felt would hinder that relationship between him and me had to go. Anything that even smelled of sin I got rid of.

There was another dimension to life that I hadn't known anything about. What I had known up to then was only the material dimension of human life. Now I was turned on to another dimension—a spiritual dimension of life, which I had just discovered to exist. It is as real as the physical life, maybe more real. And I was completely absorbed in it.

I didn't know the Bible. I didn't know Corinthians from Chronicles. So I immediately seized upon the Bible and began to read and read. It was utterly fascinating to read the things of God. This is why God did what he did—he loves us! He gave us Commandments. He walks with us. These are his purposes in history. Then I began to have a great desire to learn history because God was the God of history.

I would go to church every night that I could go. I would even sell pop bottles just to be able to take the bus to prayer services I couldn't drive to. I just wanted to be in his presence.

I took my Bible to school with me, and I would read it in study hall, in the lunchroom, wherever I could. Of course, kids would make fun of me and criticize me, but that meant nothing to me. Being ridiculed meant absolutely nothing. Schoolwork suffered because I had no interest in school or homework.

God had touched me, and all I wanted to do was to read the Bible and come to know this God who had saved me.

3

Amazing Faith

The next forty years of spiritual growth were absolutely marvelous!

You see, when the Kingdom of God comes into your heart, it dwells in your very will—not so much in your emotions—but in the will that touches your emotions. Therefore, we do what we do because we choose to do it, not because we always feel like doing it. So the Kingdom of God had totally occupied my will, and I wanted nothing else but to serve the Lord.

In that short five-minute time frame in which my conversion had taken place, I was totally changed from everything I had been to something entirely new. It brings to mind Paul's Letter to the Corinthians: "Therefore, if any one is in Christ, he is a new creation; the old has passed away, behold, the new has come" (2 Cor 5:17). That's exactly what I was—a new creation. It's not that I was born again—I've learned better since then—but it was that I had undergone a tremendous conversion, a profound spiritual experience. In that amazing moment, I had made a 180-degree turn.

My life took on a whole new existence. I was totally absorbed in the things of God. The rest of my teen years were a life of prayer and assembling with other young people who had had similar experiences. Now my idea of fun was going to a house with others like myself. We'd pray and gather around the piano and sing songs. We'd discuss Scriptures. We'd eat, pray some more, and go home.

No more hedonism for me. Now it was just life in the Spirit, and my joy was doing the will of God. There was great joy for myself and all those in my circle of friends just in doing good works. Going to hospitals and visiting the sick and praying with them brought us tremendous satisfaction. We were converted by the power of God.

When we went to worship services, I always sat in the front. I wanted to hear, listen, and see. I had an insatiable desire to understand. To this very day, that desire to learn and understand has never been satiated. I want to understand the things of God. I want to know. He is infinite and so are his workings, his purposes, his very essence and nature, what he has done and continues to do for us.

At that time I had a relationship with God, and that was the most important thing in the world to me. Nothing else mattered—nothing! I had been touched by him, and I knew that he loved me and that now I was his and he was mine. I remember those days and those nights of going to church and being totally enraptured with the things of God. Everywhere I went I took my Bible. I guess my friends thought I was a little fanatic, but it didn't matter because I had been touched by God.

I was internally driven in my quest for God. All my decisions were based on maintaining that rapport with God. I didn't break the Commandments because I knew it would be displeasing to God, and I didn't want that rapport, that relationship with God, to be broken. My relationship with God was more precious to me than anything. I believe that's what our Lord meant when he said the Greatest Commandment is to love the Lord your God with all your heart, mind, soul, and strength. That translates into a personal relationship with the Lord. And then the Second Great Commandment flows from the first: Love your neighbor as yourself. It just flows.

First Thoughts on Catholicism

But that love didn't necessarily flow to the Catholic Church in my early years. Actually, before my conversion at the age of sixteen, I didn't give the Catholic Church much thought at all. It was when I began to practice my faith after my conversion experience that I began to listen to what I was taught concerning that Church. It went something like this. The Baptists are not saved; the Methodists are not saved; the Presbyterians are not saved; the Lutherans are not saved; and the Catholics have never even started! They are the most wicked people on the face of the earth.

We were taught that Catholics actually had a hand in killing Christ because the Romans had killed Jesus, and this was the Roman Catholic Church, and somehow they were related. Catholics were not even Christians. We were taught that the Catholic Church was the great whore of Babylon as revealed in Revelation 17. It was totally and absolutely corrupt. It was like an abandoned city, haunted by dragons and unclean spirits. At one time, perhaps, it might have been viable, but now it was dead.

Every two or three months, we had a White Anglican preacher, Reverend Cross, a really down-to-earth Gospel preacher, come for a visit and a mini-revival. He was a very good man, but as I later found out, his son had been murdered by some Catholics. Whether it was over a religious issue or whether the men that murdered him just happened to be Catholic was never made clear. But every time this kindly, sincere man came, we knew it was "Catholic Night" because we knew he was going to talk about that great beast, that great whore that has corrupted every nation with her abominations. And he made it clear that the pope—with the Latin words on his tiara, which came out to 666 when translated into their numeric values—was the absolute beast. And so these ungodly beasts—these wicked priests and wicked, wicked, wicked people had martyred the saints. They had wanted to kill the godly Martin Luther, but God had protected him. And we were terrified because the book of Revelation was preached as if those events were going to happen tomorrow.

We grew up hearing and believing that the Catholic Church was the great harlot of Rome. And then we would look at how Catholics lived, and we would say: "Yup! Catholics curse more than sailors, they drink like fish, and they don't talk about Jesus. They don't read the Bible; they actually hate the Bible because it exposes them; and, in fact, they are actually forbidden to read the Bible." So we weren't even concerned about Catholics. They were beyond salvation. They were evil people and absolute apostates who hated righteousness, knew not God, persecuted the people of God, and lived in darkness. They meant nothing.

I grew up on that, and that's exactly what I believed until I went to college.

Learning, Life, and Love

I had never really considered going to college. During most of my high school days—my days of the flesh—I didn't study. So I had no desire to go to college. It was my mother who said I should go to college. She wanted me to do that. And, of course, I knew the Scriptures said to obey your mother. They also said a wise man will take instruction.

So I said, "Okay mom, I'll go to college."

I graduated from Detroit's Pershing High School in 1959, and in the winter of 1960, I started at Highland Park Junior College.

And I liked it!

I started getting As and Bs in my classes and discovered that I wasn't a moron after all! For the next five years, my college life was wonderful. I fell in love with higher learning. My only regret is that I didn't continue for my doctorate. I received a bachelor's degree in art education from Wayne State University and took graduate courses in school administration, also at Wayne State.

My college years were relatively quiet years. I loved learning, and I loved God with an unbelievable fervor. Even so, I wasn't the kind to preach my faith on a soap box. As mentioned above, I've always been somewhat of an introvert. I didn't join a fraternity or get involved in school activities. I was so much of an introvert that, believe it or not, I flunked my first speech class in college. I had very low self-esteem, and I just didn't feel like I had anything to say. But I wanted to be a teacher, and I knew I had to be able to speak in the classroom. Either you talked or you starved to death. I knew I had to come out of my introverted shell and be good at teaching and controlling the kids. It took time, and I even struggled during my first year of teaching.

I lived at home during my college years, and I took the bus to school every day. Maybe once or twice a year I was allowed to drive my mom's nice big Buick. But that was still my mom's car—she drove it, and I rode the bus like Dad. I took my classes seriously, got good grades, and also studied the Bible. My faith grew, my knowledge grew, and my understanding grew.

I had a deep love for Scripture, and the library at Wayne State had all kinds of books on the Scriptures and the prophets, so I would spend many hours there reading. I had this insatiable desire to learn Scriptures, and I never knew why. I was just driven.

Learning opened the world to me; it gave me insight into life. And I wanted to understand life because God was a God of creation and of life, and all of this was his work. And so I fell in love with my courses in politics, economics, philosophy, history—especially history—because they provided answers and the avenues to get answers.

I began to get a good insight into the historical perspective of Scripture. A lot of the things that I had begun to believe as a novice in faith, I started to realize were just interpretation. That simply fueled the flame of my desire to learn even more. So I read and read and read. Still I believed that, as a Pentecostal, my tremendous spiritual conversion had placed me on a plane where no one else lived. I was proud! But I didn't know it—that is, until an incident occurred that was very instrumental in drawing me out of my racial and spiritual prejudice.

One of my teachers, knowing I was very religious, encouraged me to attend a retreat at Highland Junior College. There were about two to three hundred people there, and nearly all were white. I remember thinking, why am I here with all these hypocrites and heathens? They certainly didn't know God! There were different Christian religions represented, including Catholics, whom still I believed to be Christ-killers.

For one of the sessions we had to pair up with someone we didn't know and sit down and dialogue with that person. I saw this little White guy, Bill, and I thought: I'll go with him, dear Lord, and show him that he needs God. So we went off to a room, and as we walked along I thought,

I'm going to jump on this boy, and I'm going to teach him the Bible. After all, I had been reading it now for at least three or four years! I decided the first thing I would deal with was the sin issue. When you're from the Pentecostal holiness background, you always deal with sin because that trips up everybody.

So I said, "You know, the Bible says that he that is born of God doth not commit sin."

And Bill said, "Yes! Because the seed is in him, and he cannot sin."

And I thought, "Hmmm. This guy knows the Bible."

Then I opened up my Bible, and he opened up his, and I was amazed because there were all kinds of Greek words in his. So I threw him a few more jabs, and he jabbed back and we began to spar. Then, all of a sudden, we just stopped, and we began simply enjoying God's Word. We began to dialogue, and we began to laugh. Have you read this? Yeah! What do you think about this?

Finally the dinner bell rang, and we had to go back with the group. We were laughing and talking, and we were having a great time. Then the thought hit me: I haven't asked what church this boy goes to.

So I said, "Bill, what church do you go to?"

And he said, "I go to Highland Park Baptist."

I said, "*Baptist?* Oh, Bill, you aren't even saved!" And he just laughed and laughed.

Then he said, "Well, when you get to heaven, Alex, you'll see me there."

I said, "Yeah, right! You need the Holy Ghost, boy! You need to speak in tongues!"

And he just laughed some more.

That moment was a moment of conversion for me—not because of what he said, but because of what he was. I saw, for a split second, that he had more Christ in him than I had in me. He had responded in love, the love of Christ, while I was trying to slit his throat spiritually. And yet he was doing nothing more than showing me the love of Christ. This produced a major crack in my theological thinking. I could actually be wrong about this guy! It was a tremendous conversion, because now I knew that I was proud. I was spiritually proud—like the Pharisees. I wasn't out committing immoral acts, but I was certainly filled with spiritual pride. And that caused me to think.

We came back with the group for dinner and were both surprised that a Catholic priest had been asked to say the blessing! Of course, it was just the beginning of my theological conversion; so when the priest finished with all of his signs and stuff, I looked at Bill and said, "Now let's bless this food properly!" And both of us prayed over the food.

School Days

After graduation, I began teaching with the Detroit Public School System in 1965. I will never forget my very first assignment. It was Schultz Elementary School in a Jewish neighborhood undergoing a cultural transition. The Chrysler Freeway was under construction during that time, and many Black families received a cash settlement for their homes and began to move into that area on the west/northwest side of Detroit.

I loved teaching elementary and junior high art there. The kids were sharp, and they could ask questions that would cause me to scramble for the answers. I enjoyed teaching those kids, but I was still very introverted. I was a very private person, and I think today, in many ways, I still am.

But when you teach in public schools, you can't be introverted. I believe that was God's means of bringing me out of my introverted ways. If he had not done that for me, I certainly would not be able to speak in front of large groups as I do today.

The second year of my teaching career and for the next four years I taught at Courville Elementary on the east side of Detroit—it was the school I had attended as a child. And it was during that second year of teaching that I met my wife Donna.

In June of 1966, I went to a retreat in Gary, Indiana. I went there to pray; to seek God; to lie before the Lord; and to get a clear idea of what God wanted me to do. My buddy, Selara Mann, came with me. We were raised in the church together. We traveled together, preached together, and evangelized together. I remember sitting there when Donna walked into the room. She was the prettiest thing I had ever seen. She was wearing a red suit with black trim, and she was absolutely beautiful! For my part, from that point on there wasn't a whole lot of praying going on.

I was twenty-five at the time and had been celibate for nine years since my conversion at the age of sixteen. I had made it relatively easy for myself by not being around women. Attraction to women was a very big weakness of mine, and I had trained myself to ignore them no matter how pretty they were. I loved the Lord so much, and I simply didn't trust myself around women. But now, I felt I was ready to get married. And it was during that service that Donna was looking mighty fine to me.

It really was love at first sight. After the prayer service, I asked if she would like some watermelon, and she said, "I hate watermelon." I thought, oh, that didn't go too well. But things got even more complicated. Her fraternal twin sister, Dianne, came into the room, and my buddy Selara was immediately taken with her. Selara began talking with Dianne. I thought Donna was my age, but she and her twin were younger than I.

In a short time, however, Selara and I were truly in love with these young women. We would drive from Detroit to Bangor, Michigan, just to be with Donna and Dianne for a few hours and then drive the 180 miles back that same day.

Eventually, we spoke with the girls' parents, and their stepfather gave us permission to marry them. He recognized that Selara and I were not scallywags, but good men who were trying to please God. He felt his daughters would be in good hands.

So on the morning of October 14, 1966, Selara and Dianne were married in Kalamazoo, and they brought Donna to me in Detroit where we were married that same evening in my pastor's home.

A year later, in August 1967, we had our first son, Joseph. The following year our second son, Benjamin, was born. Years later when the boys were teenagers, many people thought Donna was their sister.

Time of Turmoil

Life was anything but easy during our first years of marriage. That August of 1967 was the beginning of the Detroit riots. We lived on Seward and Twelfth—just two blocks from where the riots began.

I was out of the city when everything started. My brother-in-law Larry (Selara) and I were coming back home from a revival in Gary, Indiana. We were listening to gospel music on the radio when we saw the smoke rising from the city. We had no idea what was going on until we heard on the radio that there was rioting at Twelfth and Linwood. I blurted out, "Man, that's where I live!"

The police had abandoned the city, and people were looting. We saw them carrying basketsful of odd things like greens. It was nuts. Then they started with the TVs. It was a carnival atmosphere until the National Guard came in. These guardsmen were White boys from outside the city of Detroit, and they were scared to death. They were trigger-happy and ended up killing a lot of people.

The armored personnel carriers and tanks would shake the entire house as they rolled by. And when the .50-caliber machine guns would fire, the incredibly loud explosions would reverberate in our heads. Things settled down a bit after the National Guard came, but of course, they were "coon hunting", and they made no bones about it.

Donna was pregnant with Benjamin, and we were coming home from my mother's house one evening when they pulled us over. They brandished all kinds of guns, and I said, "Look, my wife is pregnant."

They just said, "Shut up and do what we tell you to do." They even had snipers on the rooftops. My wife was terrified.

One night when I came home there was a National Guardsman standing outside my home with a .45, and he said, "No one come this way—nobody!"

I said, "But I live there."

So he said, "Okay, you can park right here, but don't go any further." So I did as I was told and started to head up my stairs as another man was driving down the street.

The guardsman wielded his .45 and shouted, "Stop!" The guy didn't stop, however.

The guardsman shouted, "Stop or I'll kill you." But the guy still didn't stop.

I thought, "Oh, my God, I'm going to see this guy's brains blown all over the car!" These out-of-state guardsmen were not accustomed to ghetto neighborhoods. They were frightened and they were also trigger-happy, a bad combination.

The guardsman hollered again, "Stop or I'll blow your [expletive] brains out!"

And this guy just looked at him and slowly put his car in reverse.

I said, "Oh, thank you, God! Thank you, God! Thank you, God!"

It was a horrendous time.

In the street behind us a baby was cut in half by a .50 caliber machine gun when her father flicked a lighter to light his cigarette as he stood in front of his window. The guardsmen thought it was a muzzle flash. Bullets from a .50 caliber machine gun will go through bricks and walls like nothing, and they just cut that little girl to pieces.

It was summertime, and some evenings we would sit out on the porch. Suddenly we would hear bullets pinging off the walls right above our heads from snipers shooting at us. They would shoot at anybody—it didn't matter. So we would run into the house. Most nights we would just sleep on the floor—to protect ourselves we became accustomed to doing this during the riots.

I was doing a lot of traveling to revivals during that time. I would teach school during the week, then travel with Larry and preach on the weekends. I felt a call to do the Lord's work, but it left my very young wife alone quite a bit of the time. It was hard on her, and finally she said, "I just can't take this anymore." So we moved in with my mother and father in northeast Detroit until the riots were over.

Our third child, Marc, was born in 1972. Those were years of great trial. I didn't make a whole lot of money teaching then, and we constantly had shortfalls. I still traveled and did the Lord's work, so it wasn't easy for Donna. I have to give her a lot of credit for hanging in there. She worked part-time at nursing homes, got her GED, and started taking classes at college.

We still lived in Detroit at that time, but we had moved to a very nice middle-class area that housed a mix of White Polish and African Americans. We got along very well, although slowly the area was becoming a ghetto, and drugs started coming into the neighborhood. So Donna decided to stay home and take care of the boys.

This was, I believe, a lifesaving decision because we lived in a community that was no longer conducive to raising children. I am quite certain we would have lost all three of our boys to the streets, drugs, even death if their mother had not been there each day when they came home from school.

4

Pastor Jones

My weekends from 1966 until 1974 were often spent on the road driving to places like Chicago, Gary, and Pittsburgh. I was doing a lot of evangelical preaching and ministering while working with Mother Estella Boyd, who had been at the revival when I was fifteen and who was a spiritually gifted evangelist in the Church of God in Christ. Through her ministry I saw great healings, miracles, and workings of the Holy Spirit. It was from her that I learned the inestimable value of a consecrated life and the awesome power fervent prayer can release. I traveled with her around the Midwest for about five years and witnessed some of the most remarkable miracles I've ever seen. Needless to say, she had a tremendous impact on my own life and ministry.

I left my childhood church, Zion Congregational Church of God in Christ, in 1969 because, even though it was a good church, I believed it had become stagnant, obsolete, and trapped in following traditions irrelevant in the modern age. It was also my opinion that some in ministry there did not fully appreciate the tremendous growth of spiritual knowledge I had come to possess. I'd been exposed to fire, and I didn't like living in the smoke. I had come to understand that God's activity in the world was far above what those at Zion believed and taught. This stirred great unrest in my soul, and I felt the call of God to go build a new church community with a rising young dynamic preacher named Kenneth Collins. We bought a store front on Conant

Avenue in Detroit and literally, with our own hands, transformed that building into a church.

At the time, it seemed like a great idea, a godsend! I could become a part of what God was doing *now*, in this very generation! I had great expectations of building a church where the Kingdom of God—stripped of man-made traditions like eating the right food, wearing certain kinds of apparel, not allowing cosmetics or jewelry—could operate unhindered and unfettered. We took only the Bible as our guide and rule of life. We prayed and fasted for days at a time, all to make ourselves vessels of God's power. But after five years of selling chicken dinners at the local automotive plants, fasting until we were numb with hunger, and praying for hours on end, the church came to nothing. There was no great movement of God, no great presence of the Divine Being, no large numbers of conversions, no great masses clamoring at our doors, no great miracles, no great revival—none of the manifestations that Pentecostals expect. The venture was an absolute failure!

After that, I began suffering major lapses in my spiritual life—I got spiritually lazy. My great love for God and his work cooled dangerously. I began to have my share of failures and setbacks. Perhaps my worst failure was falling into the malaise I call *"ecclesiasticus judgmentitis"*, a spiritual condition common to churchgoers who lose their trust and faith in church leadership. The problem stemmed from my failure to put into perspective my rapid growth in knowledge. I became intoxicated with what I was learning, and, as a result, I also became arrogant and very critical and judgmental of those leaders who didn't know what I had come to know. I stopped going to church altogether, lapsing into a rebellious lukewarm state, characterized by religious indifference, bitterness toward those who were my leaders, apathy toward spiritual things in general, and a vicious fault-finding attitude that seemed to justify my hostility and, at the same time, comfort me in my misery.

Spiritual dissatisfaction always leads to personal sins, and I certainly discovered that firsthand. Those sins of the flesh that I had put behind me at my great conversion in 1958 came alive again. While I didn't return to my former life of absolute rebellion against all things religious, I surely indulged myself in self-pampering and fleshly pleasures. While Donna was very patient in urging me to go back to church, I resisted and enjoyed wallowing in self-indulgence and self-pity.

After a while I began to think, "What am I doing here?" I began to suffer with guilt and shame, and I crawled to God asking for forgiveness and help. I found out it wasn't as easy to come back as it was to leave, but through God's grace I was able to overcome this impasse in my life and come back into the church with humility.

I went back to Zion to reconnect with those who I knew loved the Lord. As much as I hated to admit it, it felt good being back home. For the next few years, I nursed my bruised ego and began growing again in the things of God. I once again enjoyed hearing good preaching, singing songs of joy and deliverance, and being with those I loved. I was very content to be home with my spiritual family, soaking up the love and acceptance that one finds particularly with such a family.

But a major point of growth and conversion had taken place before I came back to Zion. In the early 1970s I had attended a convention put on by Morris Cerullo, a Jewish convert to Christianity. He had a tremendous ministry. Going to one of his meetings I had an awakening as I began to realize how big God's Kingdom really is. To my amazement American Pentecostals were not the only ones present.

There were people from all over the world. There were Indians, Pakistanis, even folks from Scotland. It was my first exposure to the universality of the Church, and I saw that it was much bigger than what I had envisioned. My faith took a tremendous leap, and my mind expanded. So when I came back to Zion, I had grown light-years beyond the way of thinking at that church. I knew the Kingdom of God was not as we had been taught—that it was much, much different—much more inclusive.

Then, in 1974 a devastating split occurred at Zion, and that almost destroyed the church. The pastor of Zion was asked to leave because of marital problems, and the elders began seeking a new pastor. They first asked Dr. Samuel Skinner, a chiropractor and older man, who turned the offer down. Then they asked Robert Taylor, a charismatic younger man, who also declined. Finally, they asked me.

Perhaps I was the wrong man for the job, but by that time I felt I had been called to the ministry. I had been preaching for years, and I saw this as an opportunity to minister. As I felt it would be foolish to turn it down, I said yes. Before I could be ordained I had to show proficiency before the board of elders and pass an exam. After my many years of studying, all that turned out to be a snap. I was ordained in 1975 by Bishop Eddie Miller, presiding bishop of the Congregational Churches of God in Christ.

The only problem was that I was totally inexperienced as a pastor. I had never even been an associate pastor before. I didn't know anything about shepherding, feeding, or ministering to God's people; I knew nothing about administration; I was stepping in cold—ice cold.

And so began a tumultuous journey with the people of Zion. With one strike against me for leaving Zion earlier and then coming back, some perceived that I was unstable and not suitable for leadership. Yet most of the members graciously gave me the opportunity to lead them through the troubled waters of the church split. The direction I wanted to take them, however, was not the direction they wanted to go. My vision of creating an "updated" Pentecostal church, stripped of its antiquated holiness traditions and equipped with modern technology, was not exactly the vision they wanted to follow. They wanted time to regroup and heal after such a devastating split. I wanted to bring them into modern times. They wanted stability; I wanted growth. They wanted to be reaffirmed in their faith; I wanted to redefine their faith. They wanted to maintain the old Pentecostal ways and traditions of Isaiah W. Winans, their founder, but I wanted to create a ministry that reached beyond the four walls of the church and would touch the community, or better yet, the world.

Thus my first pastoral position was embroiled in tension and controversy, compounded by my lack of pastoral experience. So the struggle that ensued for the next seven-and-a-half years was understandable. I wanted to move forward, and the people of Zion wanted to fall back into the comfort of their past. They were living in a corner in their 1920s theology, and I wanted them to see the world I saw and the God I had come to know—the God who embraces people all over the world—everywhere—not just in our little Pentecostal world. I wanted them to realize that they were not the only ones God loved—that God's people were everywhere! I wanted them to understand they were not the crème de la crème. So I began to make changes.

One of the things I decided to change immediately was the communion service. Ever since I could remember, the church had had communion only twice a year. We had always been taught that communion was a very holy thing, a very sacred symbol, but a symbol nevertheless. Still, many people wouldn't even take it twice yearly because they thought it was too holy for them. After all, had not Saint Paul warned the Corinthian church, "Whoever, therefore, eats the bread or drinks the cup of the Lord in an unworthy manner will be guilty of profaning the body and blood of the Lord" (1 Cor 11:27)? In holiness churches, if one does not live up to the Commandments of God—even in minor things—taking communion is considered an act of gross misconduct.

But back then I felt that communion should be celebrated more often than twice each year, so I established a once-a-month communion service. It was a very Protestant thing to do, and I ran into a lot of difficulties implementing it because I also waived the traditional feet-washing rite that had become an integral part of the Pentecostal communion service.

I made structural changes in the church as well—redesigning the pulpit and the choir stand, doing away with some of the old furniture and bringing in the new. A huge balcony, that had accommodated several hundred worshippers in the early days of the church, had since become a heat-consuming liability—soaking up dollars in heating costs. I decided to have it covered with an arching acoustical ceiling and special lighting. It was absolutely beautiful, but it didn't go over very well.

I started a family night on Friday evenings. The goal was to provide a comfortable, joyful atmosphere with refreshments and socializing, where the adults would go to Bible study and the children to their respective areas of learning. I thought it would be a great opportunity to bring families together. But it was too new, and it didn't go over well.

Still, the small congregation at Zion grew. When I started pastoring there in 1974, I was left with about eighty-six people. That number nearly doubled in my time there. And it was during the last half of my tenure at Zion that my congregation and I witnessed amazing demonstrations of God's healing and delivering power. One of the most compelling occurred during one Sunday morning worship service.

James Hall, a rather small and slim young man of about twenty-five, walked through the front door of the church that morning and sat in the front pew directly opposite my seat in the pulpit. He was dressed quite well, wearing a light blue suit and sporting a fashionable afro. After delivering my morning sermon, I made an altar call for those who wanted salvation. He approached the altar with a small number of other respondees and stood watching me intently. I asked him if he wanted to receive Christ in his life, and he answered positively that he did, then proceeded to repeat after me the "Sinner's Prayer". After the brief prayer, I asked him to confess faith in Jesus' mercy and forgiveness, which he did, but in a rather half-hearted manner. One of my associated elders, Michael Hubbard, posed a question to him: "What do you say when someone gives you a gift?"

The young man thought a while and then responded, "Thank you?"

"Yes", Michael continued. "Now what do you say to God who has just given you the gift of eternal life?"

The young man thought about it and then said, "Thank you?"

"Yes", Michael agreed. "Now tell God thank you from your heart!"

The young man said "Thank you, Jesus" a few times, but again in a half-hearted manner.

Michael admonished him, "Say it from your heart!"

The next words from James' mouth caught everyone by surprise. He screamed, "I'm free", jumped up and down, then took off running around the entire church.

After he had run two laps around the church, I stopped him and asked, "Why are you doing this? What has happened to you?" The story he related sent chills over everyone in the church.

In his unfolding story, James told of how he had been tormented by severe depression and unresolved anger. He confessed that he had taken out his anger and depression on his family and wife, beating his wife unmercifully and at times trying to kill her. He had sought relief from doctors and other medical resources, but nothing assuaged the inner turmoil he wrestled with every day. Before coming to Zion that morning, he had loaded his shotgun and placed it in the corner of a closet, intent on killing his children, wife, and himself after worship. He had vowed that if God did not hear his prayers or deliver him from his grinding anger he would erase every vestige of himself and his family. But that day God heard his prayer and delivered him instantly from his horrific burden. Today, twenty-five years later, James is still free and preaching the Word of God at Zion. His wife and children are at his side providing spiritual and familial support.

One of the most personally rewarding moments of my time as pastor of Zion was when my father came back to church. He was always a good man, but without any formal religion. I had never seen my dad enter a church until I became the pastor in 1976. He came forward during an altar call. I was so surprised that I asked, "Why are you here? Are you here to be saved?"

He answered, "Yes." And I just cried.

I baptized my own father, and he became a regular at church services and prayer meetings. And I eulogized him when he died in 1980. I know I'll see him again.

In spite of such amazing works of the Holy Spirit, as the years went on that nagging hunger to be on the cutting edge of God's work resurfaced. I felt we were not having much success in reaching our generation. So with one of my fellow ministers, Leon White, I went to the mean streets of Detroit to share the good news of the Gospel. We walked up and down Gratiot and Woodward avenues sharing the Word with all who would stop and listen. Unfortunately, those we brought to the church made the existing members uncomfortable, and so they cautioned us that "those kinds of people don't belong here!" That demonstration of prejudice against certain "kinds" of people, combined with my growing knowledge of the inclusive nature of God's Kingdom, created unrest in my heart again.

In hindsight, it might have been better to have said no to Zion's invitation to pastor them. After twenty-five years of pastoring, I now understand that they needed a more seasoned and gentle pastor to come in for a while and leave things untouched. They needed someone who could bring healing to a wounded congregation, a man of gentler gifts who could work with them and slowly restore their spiritual health.

By this time I had discovered and embraced Evangelical Christianity. There weren't too many books written by Pentecostals that had any real scholarship or literary depth; most dealt with spiritual principles or spiritual experiences. In fact, anything intellectual was considered "carnal" or "man-made" and unworthy of pursuit. But my college years had opened a door of intellectual curiosity, and I increasingly understood that God's creation of the human mind was being grossly neglected by those who feared and criticized anything intellectual or historical. To those I associated with, the Scriptures were the bread and meat of man's existence. Nothing was worthy of pursuit or study with the exception of "scriptural truths". Needless to say, my intellect was neither challenged nor fed, and I became increasingly hungry for anything that was scholarly or intellectually stimulating. Consequently, I began reading everything I could get my hands on that threw greater light on the human condition and the flow and development of mankind.

I began reading biblical history, Old and New Testament theology, the historical development of Protestantism from Luther and Calvin, and the great doctrines of Evangelical Christianity. Here my grasp of the Christian faith began to find an intellectual foundation: we are saved by faith through grace, not by legalistic ordinances or traditions! The all-encompassing work of Calvary had set us free from legal obligations—we are free from condemnation and heaven is our eternal home. We can know we are saved here and now!

While I never fully accepted the Evangelical concept of eternal security, I was excited and intellectually invigorated to discover Evangelical teachings. The Bible came alive with new and wonderful truths that Pentecostals had somehow overlooked. The spiritual experiences they had provided were indeed powerful, but their grasp of biblical truth was lacking scholarship and intellectual scrutiny. Pentecostals' bias against intellectual scholarship had left them floundering in a variety of scriptural interpretations that often bordered on the bizarre and ridiculous. Pentecostals had indeed rediscovered the life-changing baptism into the Holy Spirit, but they had fallen flat in biblical scholarship and theological development.

By 1982, I decided to leave that church because I felt I would be doing more damage by staying there. I know a lot of people were hurt by my decision to leave. I had attracted new people to the church, and some of the older people had really grown to love me. And so it was painful when it came time to say good-bye. Some of them just cried. But then, there were others who rejoiced: "He's finally out of here!" Although I didn't ask anyone to come with me when I left, some of them did. In many ways, it was the saddest day of my life; I had to leave behind many good people who loved me, but would not come with me. It was painful to walk away from the church that had birthed and nurtured me, but there was no turning back.

I started Maranatha (Aramaic for "Lord, come") Christian Assembly in October 1982, along with about twenty families from Zion. And so began eighteen years of pastoring a church of wonderful, God-fearing, God-loving, good people.

Our first church building was an old abandoned bar in Highland Park. We knew the man who owned the building and asked if we could rent it for a church. He rented it to us for $300 a month. So we partitioned the bar off, carpeted the floor, built the pulpit and platform, put some nice chairs in there, and even had a little kitchenette. It turned out well.

We stayed there for a year before we bought a ten-thousand-square-foot Amway warehouse at Six Mile Road and Woodward Avenue in Detroit. We had some great workers in our little congregation, and we managed to raise the $36,000 cash needed to purchase the building. That was our church home for the next three years.

In our fourth year of existence, we bought the church on Oakman Boulevard in Detroit. It was a beautiful, white-domed, spacious and ornate, former Greek Orthodox church building, and I changed our name to Maranatha Christian Church. It would be our church home for the next fourteen years—until Maranatha was no more.

When I first started Maranatha, I felt I was finally free, that I could really begin making some changes. I was euphoric. I thought I had the freedom to present the Gospel as I now understood it, reshaped in the image of Evangelical Christianity. At Zion I had been inhibited by the local traditions of that congregation. There were prohibitions against things like wearing shorts, jewelry, or cosmetics; the consumption of any alcohol whatsoever; dancing; watching movies; card-playing; and even playing checkers. With the organization of Maranatha, I could at last do away with these anachronistic traditions and minister the Gospel as I had come to know it. I could preach the Gospel of freedom and grace, "not because of works, lest any man should boast" (Eph 2:8). The "legalistic traditions" of the Pentecostal holiness movement would be a thing of the past! I was free to preach an "Evangelical Gospel", a Gospel of grace, with such coteries as John McArthur, Chuck Swindoll, Chuck Smith, the late Doctor J. Vernon McGee, and Charles Stanley. I could now blend my Pentecostal experiences with Evangelical theology and produce a powerful Gospel of inclusion that was rooted in spiritual power and the written Word of God. But there was a flaw.

The flaw in my planning was my failure to understand the needs of the people who had come with me. They were traditional Pentecostals who wanted progress, but with qualifications. While they wanted progressive teachings, they wanted them within the context of Pentecostal theology and practice. They were basically of the same mindset as those I had left, yet they came with me because they loved me and interpreted my "progressiveness" to be an "updating of Pentecostalism", not what I had really intended and envisioned during my time at Zion—a blending of the Pentecostal experience with Evangelical theology. So when I began to implement changes in my new church, changes that reflected my knowledge of the Gospel, they said, "You've changed."

Indeed, I *had* changed. I was really being me now. I wanted to get away from what I knew to be Pentecostal provincialism and extremism and move into a more Evangelical worship with its corollary: emphasis on expository biblical teaching. Throughout Maranatha's existence I would periodically feel the need at least to *try* to realize my vision of a charismatic/Evangelical ministry encompassing social outreach in the community. I would make changes, but almost every time I would have to back off because of the cool reception from my congregants. I created hymnals to replace the traditional extemporary call-and-response songs typical of congregational singing. That fell like a dud! Hymnals were something foreign to our traditional Pentecostal spirituality, and using them just didn't work!

I also began to recognize the need to be more socially conscious—to be concerned about *all* of God's children. I had grown to understand that the Christian message demanded more than spiritual experiences and dynamic worship; the Gospel message demanded change within *society* as well as changes within the human heart. But that would not become a reality at Maranatha because the emphasis never shifted from worship to ministry. The question that we should have been asking, "How do we change society?" became "Why do we worship as we do?"

Yet good things happened at Maranatha. Along with the fellowship, love, and caring, healings took place there too. One healing that occurred in October 1989 was confirmed by medical science.

Zelma Hubbard, wife of my associate pastor, Michael Hubbard, became ill in January 1988. The disease was originally diagnosed as the adult onset of juvenile rheumatoid arthritis (Still's disease). The condition devastated Zelma and left her in agonizing pain with decreasing mobility. Her pain and disability eventually caused her to be housebound, with occasional visits to the store and even more rarely to church. After two weeks in the hospital, the disease was finally identified as systemic lupus erythematosus (SLE). For eighteen months, Zelma suffered excruciating pain and discomfort in all of her joints, including her feet, hands, and even in the joints of her fingers. Finding it too painful to get up, Zelma became bedridden and increasingly depressed because she was unable to function as a wife and mother. Her involvement in church work came to a halt, her job with the Army's Corps of Engineers was placed on hold, and a once-vibrant life began to wither away in pain and immobility. The doctors began with aspirin therapy, changed to steroid infusions, and eventually ended with giving Zelma the oral steroid Prednisone for a year. Nothing worked. Zelma only gained weight from the steroids until she became obese and disfigured in her appearance. Zelma was a constant object of our prayers for healing and deliverance.

Eighteen months later, in October 1989, God completely healed Zelma. As she lay in her bed crying and asking God for his healing touch, all the pain suddenly went away. She literally leaped out of bed and began touching her toes and doing jumping jacks! At her next doctor's visit, Zelma shocked the doctor by jumping off the examination table and performing jumping jacks for him. The doctor was astounded, calling the incident a remarkable remission of the disease. Zelma remains symptom-free to this day.

In spite of all the good that happened at Maranatha from the opening day in October 1982, until the church building was sold in July 2000, the Maranatha ministry never really achieved its intended purpose. In hindsight I see now that I did not possess the necessary pastoral gifts to bring about such a significant change, yet I was a good pastor because I loved my people and did the best I could in shepherding them and sharing with them the truths of the Gospel.

To comply with Saint Paul's admonition that "all things should be done decently and in order" (1 Cor 14:40), I increasingly stressed a well-thought-out, structured worship program, but that too was coolly received because many believed it "stifled" the freedom of the Spirit.

Frustrated in my attempts to combine Evangelical theology with Pentecostal experience, I increasingly felt obligated to make adjustments for my congregation because, after all, the members were good people who had sacrificed much to support my ministry and I couldn't risk the possibility of driving them away. Of course, the frequent attempts at something new would lead them to think, "Pastor's on a new change binge again!" Unfortunately, such concessions gave them the impression that I was unstable and without a vision. I knew I wasn't unstable, but frustrated and torn between trying to realize my vision of the Gospel and yet do it in such a way so as not to alienate those who sat in the pews. It did not work, and I came away looking indeed like a pastor without a vision, frustrated and driven by every whim and impulse.

Of course, it wasn't all bad. The Maranatha years, overall, were wonderful years of growth and maturity as we slowly coalesced into a warm community of caring believers. Although I still had to carry vestiges of that old Pentecostal image, at least I had more freedom than I did in my first church.

Even though we never grew to be a large church (we had about two hundred members at our peak), and although there were occasional struggles with my attempts at change, the Maranatha family was a great place to experience a well-grounded Christian community. Despite the increasingly obvious fact that I would never realize my dream, I nevertheless found consolation and satisfaction in teaching and preaching the truths of the Gospel, shepherding my flock, and watching my people grow and mature in their Christian endeavors.

Photo 1. Alex Clarence Jones, Sr., circa 1920.

Photo 2. Alex at 18 months to 2 years with his mother Margaret Jones and sister Gwen. Photo circa 1943.

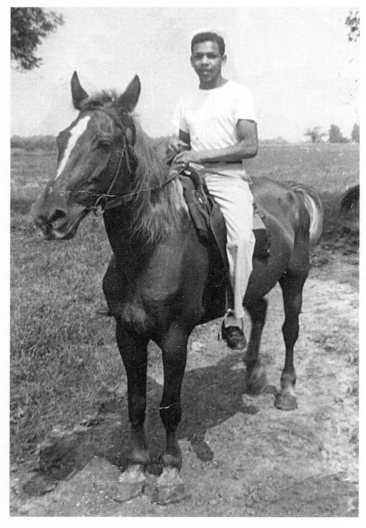

Photo 3. Alex at 15 riding on horseback in Chatham, Ontario, Canada.

Photo 4. Graduation from Pershing High School in Detroit
on June 16, 1959.

Photo 5. Alex, 18, in 1959.

Photo 6. Alex and Donna Jones are married at a pastor's home in Detroit.

Photo 7. Alex and his dad in the early 1970s.

Photo 8. Gwen, Harold, and Alex in the early 1970s.

Photo 9. Alex (in front) with (from left) his dad Alex, Sr., his brother Harold, his mother Margaret, a family friend, and his sister Gwen.

Photo 10. Taking part in a religious television broadcast in the mid-1970s.

Photo 11. Pastor of Zion Congregational Church of God in Detroit in the late 1970s.

5

Family Life

Donna has always been a phenomenal mother to our three boys, Joseph, Benjamin, and Marc. And raising children in Detroit during the 'seventies and 'eighties was a phenomenal task. I have no doubt that her love, dedication, and skills as a mother—being there for them, teaching them, praying with them, and putting the fear of God into them at a very young age—have much to do with the fact that they grew into fine, upstanding, respectable young men. Their teen years, however, marked a very tumultuous period in all of our lives.

The boys sometimes associated with the wrong people. The neighborhood we then lived in was deteriorating rapidly. Almost every night there were gunshots, bursts of automatic fire—people trying out new weapons. Often Donna would sleep on the floor at night, fearful that a stray bullet might pierce the walls of our home. It was part of life. Most people don't realize what goes on in the inner city; they don't have any idea. It seemed like a war zone. We lived on the northeast side of Detroit, which, in the fifties and sixties, had been a respectable, multicultural neighborhood of Polish and African Americans, but in the seventies and eighties had deteriorated into a drug-dealing, violence-ridden community. A number of my sons' friends were injured or murdered on the streets of Detroit during the 1970s and 1980s. My saddest moments as a pastor were officiating at funerals of young Black men whose lives were snuffed out by mindless street violence. Some were killed by shotgun because they were at the wrong place at the wrong time; others died under a hail of bullets from submachine guns because they accidentally "bumped" into someone. One tragic funeral that vividly stands out in my mind was for one of my son's friends who died in his father's arms, shot while he was trying to mediate an argument between two men.

This was a rough time, a time when we truly learned the power of prayer. When the phone rang at night, we didn't want to pick it up. And we never knew when the police might knock on our door and say they had found one of our sons dead. We lived with that fear constantly hanging over our heads. Whenever our boys went off to school or were out after dark—we just never knew.

We realized our children were in danger, but I didn't make enough money to move out of the community. I made anywhere from $200 to $500 a month as a pastor, and I didn't make much as a teacher—just enough to pay the bills and get by.

So I had a talk with the Lord and said, "Look, I don't have a whole lot of money, and that's fine with me; I don't desire to be wealthy. I don't require fame and glory; that is absolutely meaningless to me. The only thing I ask of you is to just give me my family. Just protect them in this city of violence and take care of them." And he did.

Donna and I did a lot of praying for our kids. That's why we are so acutely aware of the power of prayer. We had to pray to survive. It wasn't an option. What other recourse did we have? We had the greatest power in the universe at our disposal, so we used it. That's why I believe the faith of poor people is often so much stronger than that of people who have all their needs met. Poor folks rely on their relationship with God. Look at the great saints. They gave up their wealth to become poor, because it is in poverty that one truly knows the power of God. Jesus pointed out how hard it is for a rich man to enter into the Kingdom of heaven. That is because often he has no needs; he relies on his own wealth. There is no fear, no need to trust.

So Donna and I learned to rely on the Lord. We raised our three boys in that environment and, thanks be to God, they weren't killed. They did, however, get into their share of trouble—some of it serious. Several times there were run-ins with the law. Sometimes deserved, other times not. Sometimes racism was a factor.

I thank God that none of my kids got involved in taking drugs. Ironically, my only brother, Harold—a half-brother who was eight years older than me—was a big-time drug dealer and supplier. He was very smart, but always a person of the world. While he loved the life of the world, family was very important to him. He loved our mother more than life, and Mom loved him intensely too. She fasted and prayed that God might save him.

Harold also loved our boys and didn't want them in any way associated with drugs. But when one of our boys, Ben, was about twenty and traveling in the car with Harold, they were stopped by policemen and arrested on trumped-up charges. The only thing that saved my son from prison was my brother's plea-bargaining. He pleaded guilty on a lesser charge.

"I believe I could've beaten this charge," Harold later told me, "but if I had lost, it would have meant a prison term for Ben. He didn't do anything to deserve this, and I wanted him to go free." So Harold was sent to a federal prison where he died from cancer about a year later.

During those child-rearing years, there were times that were so distressing it just tore at my heart. Donna and I relied on guidance from the Lord in the actions we took. A number of times I had to go and get the boys from very unsavory places. One evening I found my oldest son at a raucous teen party held in a small club so crowded it was amazing anyone could move. Yet through the hazy smoke, blaring music, and undulating bodies I saw my son Joseph dancing the night away. I wouldn't have minded had it just been a gathering of teens having some good clean fun, but this was an illegal gathering of teens that included drugs and plenty of booze.

Then there was Luomo's, a popular gathering place for teens on Seven Mile Road, which also, unfortunately, attracted "dead-enders"—school dropouts who came armed and looking for confrontations. Again and again I had to go to Luomo's to retrieve first one son and then another. I would go into these clubs and hang-outs and tell them, "You have to leave here now—this is not a decent place to be."

Of course, I did it out of love. I refused to give up on them, even if I had to put myself in danger to get them. I tried teaching them, but they often didn't want to listen. I chastised and disciplined them, but sometimes it seemed to no avail. Being a preacher brought some respect, but not enough for them to live by my standards. When I asked them to leave a situation, even though they didn't want to go, they did because they respected me. Sometimes they would go back there again, and I would, once again, retrieve them. Free will was something Donna and I understood, but didn't always appreciate. As a father, I would not let my children go without a struggle; they were *my* children, *my* flesh and blood, part of *my* body. I would suffer whatever it took to redeem them, to save them from destruction, to bring them to spiritual health and happiness. Then, and only then, did I fully understand the Cross.

It was through these painful experiences that I came to understand the heart of God. I understood with increasing clarity the aching heart of a father whose son rejects his authority and chooses to live in a far country rather than his father's house. Through these often excruciating experiences of having my standards of Christian life rejected by my sons, their increasing attraction to the world and the sins of the flesh, and their headlong rush to perdition, I came to know the depth of God's love for us. It was then that I fully appreciated the fact that God is not some heavenly tyrant issuing threats of doom and destruction or scribbling notes for some future punishments, but he is a father like me, hurt by his children's rejection, yet constantly pursuing them with a love so perfect and so complete that it cannot be comprehended, it can only be accepted and appropriated. Saint Paul said it best when he wrote: "God shows his love for us in that *while we were yet sinners Christ died for us*" (Rom 5:8, italics are mine).

I believe those experiences helped to prepare me in my ministry. In some respects, that was part of my formation. I could relate to people in a variety of situations, including the heartbreak of difficulties with children. I could understand parents' hearts being broken because my own heart and my wife's heart had been broken many, many times.

The boys have sometimes asked me how their mother and I were able to deal with them during those years. Looking back, I can see clearly how it was the grace of God that carried us through those difficult times. And God has answered our prayers many times over. All three of our sons are now married to wonderful women, and we have eight beautiful grandchildren.

Joseph is a construction management consultant and works for a company in Detroit as well as with his brothers in real estate. He is married to Bianca, and they have two young children; Joseph, Jr., and Alexes. Joe is also taking classes at Sacred Heart Major Seminary in Detroit, working on his theology degree.

Benjamin, the one who as an adolescent gave me the most trouble and cause for tears, now sees the light. He has expressed a deep desire to minister to those who still live on the mean streets of Detroit. He currently works along with his brothers—refurbishing houses and putting them back on the market. Ben and his wife Tamala have a daughter Tamiia. Ben also has two children from before he was married: D'Andre—twenty, and Camille—nineteen.

Marc works at Chrysler as well as in restorative real estate. He is married to Caleetha, and they have three young daughters, Lauren, Catherine, and Candice Ebony. Marc is a National Guardsman and served three-and-a-half months in Iraq during the spring of 2004. (He returned to his family on July 25, 2004.)

God has more than answered our prayers. He gave us our family—he kept them safe. He has honored our plea by taking care of the greatest blessings in our lives. And he has given us a very special blessing that I am most thankful for. All of my children and all except for one grandchild, entered the Catholic Church along with me.

6

Changing Thoughts

During most of my eighteen years of pastoring at Maranatha, Catholicism remained the furthest thing from my mind. After seven years as pastor there, I retired from my job as a middle school teacher and, from that point, devoted myself full-time to the church.

As the years progressed, I became increasingly aware that the Christian message was far more than just the shout, the euphoric feelings of spiritual experiences, and speaking in tongues. Those things were good, but I felt that in too many Pentecostal circles these had *replaced* the end of all spiritual and mystical experiences, which is to bring the Kingdom of God into the community in which one lives. Unfortunately, the pursuing of spiritual experiences had turned many inward, causing them to be overly concerned with their personal relationship with Christ. The very concept of the church as community seldom got beyond what was good for the individual, that is, what each one got out of his church. This individualistic pursuit of spiritual satisfaction was often the basis for the "church-hopping" so characteristic of members of nondenominational churches. Pentecostalism was indeed a *vibrant* faith offering a powerful encounter with the Holy Spirit, a deepened spiritual conversion that brought with it an intuitive knowledge of and hunger for God,[1] a heightened familiarity with the

[1] Jeremiah 31:31–34 describes the nature of the New Covenant God would enter into with his people. The heart and soul of this New Covenant would

presence of Jesus within, and an enlightened approach to the Bible as the powerful Word of God. Yet, the Christian message demanded much, much more. It demanded bringing the Kingdom of God into every aspect of human affairs, challenging, building, and sanctifying society.

I loved the people at Maranatha and wanted to accommodate them and meet their spiritual needs, but by the same token, because I knew there was more—that the Gospel message contained more than soulful praise, moving worship, and Bible knowledge—I also wanted to move them beyond those aspects. Unfortunately, my ministry never developed that social dimension. It remained a Bible-based ministry that taught spiritual principles, but was barren of any real ministry to others.

At least we had gotten away from the extreme form of Pentecostalism I had experienced in my youth. That Pentecostalism taught a very virulent form of racism—that Whites just couldn't be saved. They were unsalvageable because of the brutal form of slavery to which they had subjected our fathers. It also taught a very extreme form of elitism that condemned all Christian denominations outside of our particular brand of Pentecostalism as unholy and unworthy of God's acceptance. Baptists, Methodists, Presbyterians (Catholics weren't even considered) were lost. As I matured in my faith, it didn't take long for me to see that the things we were taught were unscriptural and didn't make sense. Slowly and methodically, the Holy Spirit began to

---

be the *interiority* of God himself whereby the covenanted people of God would share in his divine life. This knowledge of God would spring from within as an intuitive familiarity of his life, his person, and his will (Rom 12:2; 1 Cor 2:10–13). Such knowledge could not be obtained through study or reflection, but through the active presence of the Spirit within.

lead me into an understanding of the inclusiveness of God's Kingdom.

Much of my change in thinking came about because of what I read and understood and, of course, because of life experiences. I have always loved to read—the Bible, scholarly works, anything imparting knowledge. From the time of my conversion on that hot August night, I have had an insatiable appetite for the Scriptures and to learn about God's actions in history. The more I read, the more I came to understand that many Pentecostal beliefs were untenable scripturally and inaccurate historically. Although I was raised in the Pentecostal faith, I moved slowly from that very biased, prejudicial, provincial faith to a more inclusive faith, stopping for a time at Evangelical Christianity—far short of Catholicism.

What turned me around and thoroughly scourged me of extreme forms of Pentecostal worship, however, was one particular service I attended as a young adult. I was trying to get into the Spirit and was clapping my hands while people all around me were screaming and shouting and rolling on the floor. One brother was trying to climb the wall, another actually put his foot through his chair—boom! I just stopped and looked at all these things going on, and I thought, "If someone had just found Christ, wanted to learn more about him, and walked in at this very moment, what would they think?" I had no doubt that they would think we were all crazy!

I approached my church leaders and asked where we find this type of worship in Scripture. I even asked my pastor why the Holy Spirit never seemed to show up in great power until midway through his sermon when he asked everyone to say Yes. It had become apparent to me that the spiritual power released at our initial encounter with the Holy Spirit had settled into the highly emotional Pentecostal tradition of call-and-response worship. That apparently was not the kind of questioning to which the church leaders were accustomed. It angered them, and they said, "Who are you to question us?" They told me, "You read too much, and your reading is affecting the way you think. You have to let the Lord lead you." But I never allowed that kind of free-spirit worship at Maranatha. In fact, if people got too ecstatic, I would stop them. After all, Paul wrote to the Corinthians, "So, my brethren, earnestly desire to prophesy, and do not forbid speaking in tongues; but all things should be done decently and in order" (1 Cor 14:39–40).

While I had experienced real spiritual power in the Pentecostal church—life-transforming power—some of what I saw was more of a showy type of thing, more like entertainment. I saw how a few Pentecostal pastors and preachers were little more than psychological manipulators. They knew what to say to get people excited, and they were extremely good at it. But when I began to examine what they were saying and doing, much of it consisted of empty promises that fired people up, but had a negligible impact on the communities in which they lived.

That was particularly evident when it came to the idea of prosperity. "God wants you to be prosperous", the preacher would intone in a loud booming voice. Preachers would create a hodgepodge theology using 3 John 1:2 with Deuteronomy 28 and other Old Testament Scriptures to show that God wants you healthy, wealthy, and wise. And if you're sick, poor, or unwise, it's because you don't know the Word or you don't have enough faith. Over the years I came to understand that the prosperity message was a perversion of the Gospel of Jesus Christ. It was a "bastardization" of the paradoxical message of the Gospel that one gains life by dying (Mt 10:38–39) and prospers by sacrificing (Mt 19:21). The Gospel of Jesus Christ entails suffering, and suffering is redemptive. I didn't know it to the extent that Catholic theology teaches, but I knew that our sufferings weren't caused by the devil riding our backs.

Many of my brethren were teaching that you need to get the devil off your back and stand up—that God wants you to control your circumstances. Here I was thinking, "No, God wants you to be controlled by him." I had come to understand that our relationship with Christ was built upon loving trust and obedience and had nothing to do with our own controlling of our circumstances or calling things into being that do not exist. I knew the real victory in our relationship with God was over doubt and despair in our sufferings, and being steadfast in our many temptations. I knew there was another side of faith as glorious as the faith that delivers out of trouble—the faith that remains strong in trouble. I knew that true faith is remaining loyal to our Lord when we don't understand, when our circumstances are almost unbearable, and when our sufferings give no indication of God's love and grace.

I would preach often that the prosperity message was not the Gospel of Jesus Christ; it was not the *kerygma* (proclamation of religious truths) preached by the apostles: prosperity has nothing to do with the Gospel. Some of my congregants got tired of hearing me say that. They didn't want to hear it. Many liked hearing that God wants you wealthy. It was *name it and claim it; blab it and grab it!*

I tried to explain to them that that way of thinking was an abuse of the Christian message. It was clear in the Scriptures that the saints and the apostles sought to empty themselves—not to be filled with power and wealth, but to

be filled with the humility of the Lord, to be servants[2]
(Greek, *doulos*, slaves) of God.

Once I discovered that perhaps what many Pentecostals
believed and taught was not totally correct, I desired to
read even more. I recognized that their knowledge was good
as far as moral teaching, but when it came to historical
facts and the exegesis of Scripture—they fell short. I realized that the extreme form of Pentecostal worship was atyp-
ical and not the worship of the Church. It had never been.
So that was my break with traditional Pentecostalism.

But the folks who came with me as part of my initial
Maranatha congregation still wanted Pentecostal worship and
beliefs, and, by this time, I was becoming more Evangelical
than Pentecostal. They wanted the moving of the Spirit.
They wanted the Holy Ghost to fall. They wanted the gifts
of the Spirit to operate. They wanted me to operate the
gifts of the Spirit, while I simply wanted to declare the
message of the Gospel with newfound clarity.

I tried to explain, "Hey, I'm not that kind of person. I'm
a teacher. I'm a preacher. I'm a leader. I'm not a miracle-
worker or healer. The apostles had ecstatic experiences in
the Upper Room, but they came out of the Upper Room,
and they won the world. Why do you want to stay in the
Upper Room?"

So, for me, the Pentecostal teachings became secondary.
Some were good, but they were secondary. What was pri-
mary was the *evangelion*—the good news of the Gospel; getting people to hear what God had *for* them and wanted
from them; getting out of that church and into the community; letting people know God will change their lives.

[2] Paul refers to himself as a *doulos* of Jesus Christ (Rom 1:1; Gal 1:10).
Jesus was the perfect example (Phil 2:7).

That sounds easy, but that's a hard thing to get Christians to do.

Many times I would go out into the neighborhoods with my chairman of the deacon board, Clarence Ewing. We would create teams and go out and knock on doors and tell people about the Lord. That's why I had such a great respect for him; he put his faith into action. He was with me all the way. "Brother Pastor," he would say, "I understand. I'll go with you." And he did go with me. Clarence Ewing was a holy man, a good man. Whenever I held a prayer service, he was there. He always loved to pray. When we prayed at the church at six o'clock every Sunday morning, he was one of the first ones there. When we went into the community, he was there. That's why it was so hard when we eventually parted. It was especially painful after my decision to become Catholic when he said, "I can't walk with you anymore."

So, even though I had more freedom at Maranatha, it was not complete freedom. And it was in that freedom that I lost the respect of a lot of people by what they perceived as flip-flopping—urging them to change and then trying to accommodate the way they wanted things. Because of that I wasn't able to move them in the direction I knew to be true. I felt I had to draw back. I was not fully free, and they were not fully satisfied. Perhaps that is one of the reasons why some of my congregants wouldn't come with me when I did enter the Catholic Church. They likely thought, "Oh, this is just another move for change Pastor Alex is making."

Periodically our church would go on retreat at Colombière, a Jesuit retreat center in Clarkston, Michigan. We had men's and couple's retreats there, and I would talk to the men from the lectern next to the altar. Even at that time, I always felt there was something special there. I knew that in some way the Catholic Church was connected to early Christianity, but like so many others, I viewed Catholicism as a mere historical relic that had lost its way through a fossilized formalism that had driven the Holy Spirit from its pews. Yet, I recall feeling a little uncomfortable because somehow I was not really connected to the past, even though our vibrant faith had brought us into a deep, personal relationship with God. The beautiful statuary and crucifixes adorning the chapel touched me in some strange way, but our faith would never allow those "graven images" and crucifixes to adorn *our* sanctuary. Even though I rejected the Catholic context in which I saw them, I must admit that I was drawn to them and felt a certain kinship with them.

I knew nothing about the Catholic Church and had no desire to learn about it then. I just knew that this was a special holy place. I would see people come in just to pray, and I thought that was great. Beholding the crucifix, I knew this was a serious place where the crucifixion of Christ was recognized. And I would feel in my heart, "There is a palpable reverence in this place, and I'd like to worship here." I had often felt God should be honored as a great king, and, at times, the Christian worship should be done silently. But silence was deadly to Pentecostalism. One had to clap hands and make some noise.

During our retreats at Colombière, however, I would sometimes slip into those little chapels with the private altars and close the door and pray. I think those times at Colombière were the beginnings of contemplative prayer for me. Those times of quiet meditative prayer in those small cubicles were profoundly influential in my prayer life. I really wanted to know God, draw near to God, and, especially, to honor God properly.

All these thoughts were going through my mind even before I read the Church Fathers for the second time. I wasn't really able to share all that I had come to understand because when I would try to share part of it I would hear, "There he goes again!" So a lot of what I knew I kept within my heart. And as I got older, I felt as though my life was passing by, and I never would have a chance really to preach those things. I was in my fifties then, and by 1994 I was looking forward to retirement. I felt that I should begin constructing the church so that it could continue without me.

In fact, by 1996, I just wanted to quit. I was tired of the struggle, tired of the problems, and I was burned out. I didn't care any more about getting my message across. I thought about retiring early and teaching at a university. I contacted Wayne State University in Detroit about taking courses for my master's degree. I worked with a counselor, and we had about two years of courses all mapped out for me. I was to start on a Monday for the spring 1997 semester, but the night before classes were to begin, it seemed that the Holy Spirit was telling me not to do this.

About three o'clock in the morning, I went into the living room to pray. While I was praying it seemed as though the Lord began to speak to my heart and say: *Alex, you never really trusted me or came to me for your strength. You always tried to do things yourself. You leaned on yourself and trusted your own strength and your own wisdom. You know, I've always been there for you.* I began to cry. And, from that experience, the Lord began to renew me. I asked for his peace and asked him to forgive me.

Then the peace of God that is indescribable and the joy of the Lord began to fill my heart and soul. He had renewed me, and I knew I could begin pastoring once again. I cancelled all my classes, and the following Sunday I shared my

experience with my congregation. I said that I had been
burned out, but the Lord had renewed me. And I continued as pastor there for another four years, fulfilling the work
I felt God had called me to do—and work that I enjoyed—
preaching, visiting with families, marrying, burying, counseling, and teaching the good people of Maranatha.

In fact, it was teaching the Wednesday evening Bible study
there that launched my journey into the Catholic Church.

7

The Joy of Discovery

I have always loved teaching the Bible—absolutely loved it! And it was early in 1998, shortly after that experience of being renewed, when we began reading Paul's epistles to Timothy in our Wednesday evening Bible study. Our midweek study, held in a classroom at the church, was well attended, with anywhere from thirty to forty adults present.

People loved it. We had classes for kids too. I would try different techniques in order to teach with clarity—so that those I was teaching would really understand Scripture and what was happening in that time period. I loved taking the Word of God and peeling it open to get the essence of it—not just the historical aspects of the Word, but the existential aspects of it—how it impacts us now. Sometimes I would use the blackboard or the overhead projector. Sometimes we would break up into discussion groups, and other times we would pray and sing songs. I would take a theme and develop that theme for a few weeks, or I would take a book of the Bible and teach it for a few months.

For this study, we began with Paul's First Letter to Timothy because it had a lot of information about teaching doctrine, Church, the life of the believer—a wealth of good theological material. We studied chapter 1 for about two weeks, and it went very well. Then we came to chapter 2, which deals with public prayer and public worship. In that chapter Paul spoke about men praying for those in authority—for kings and governors; praying or lifting holy hands without wrath or doubting; about women being silent in church, and not usurping authority over men. The latter was something I really wanted to bring out because I thought women were getting a bad rap for that.

I wanted to talk about what intercessory prayer really was, about what worship was. Paul was sharing with Timothy how to lead the Church in corporate worship. So I came up with what I thought was a great idea. Why not simply experience what the early Church experienced? Why not just recreate this first-century worship service so we could all understand how it was done two thousand years ago? I thought this would be something we would never forget—that it would impress on all of us exactly how the early Church operated. I had no clue just how prophetic my thoughts were.

So I asked my class, "How would you like to get into a time machine and go back two thousand years to the time of the early Church?" The participants liked the idea. They thought it was quite novel. So when they said yes, I said, "Give me a month." I knew I would need to do a little research.

I had no idea that I would be finding anything new. I had read Church history and some of the early Church Fathers before. And I knew that in order to get the proper perspective of the Church in its infancy, I would need to read not only the Bible but also the works of these men who had known the apostles or who had been closest to the apostles—to that first generation.

I was intrigued by these men. I thought they were rather eccentric and a bit extreme since they hadn't agreed with my way of thinking, but I knew they had valuable historical information. I had inklings that the Eucharist played an important part in early worship services, but I wasn't quite sure exactly what the Eucharist was.

When I came home that evening, the first thing I did was to get on the Internet and type in "Church Fathers". I wanted to start at the beginning. I knew what the Bible said about worship, but I needed to expand my research to the earliest writers of the Christian faith. I quickly discovered that the writings of the Church Fathers covered a seven-hundred-year period of Church history, from A.D. 90 to A.D. 750, and I had to narrow my search to those Fathers who either knew the apostles or knew the first disciples of the apostles. These apostolic Fathers were Saint Clement of Rome (d. 96), the third bishop of the Roman Church who knew Saint Peter; Saint Ignatius of Antioch (50–107), the second bishop of Antioch who knew Saint John; Saint Polycarp of Smyrna (66–155), who was a disciple of Saint John; and the anonymous authors of the *Didache*; *Shepherd of Hermas*; the *Epistle of Barnabas*; and the *Fragment of Papias*. With these documents in hand, the weeks that followed became an amazing journey, leading to the truth that would change my life forever.

Once I began reading the seven letters of Ignatius of Antioch,[1] I came face to face with authentic Christianity as it had been handed down from the apostles to the first generation of bishops. Saint Ignatius, with the echo of apostolic teaching still ringing in his ears, urged Christians to pursue spiritual maturity and that holiness of life without which no one shall see the Lord. He exhorted his fellow Christians to be God-bearers[2] and to grow in holiness of

[1] Seven letters have been recognized as authentically written by Ignatius of Antioch: his public letters to the Ephesians, Magnesians, Romans, Philadelphians, Smyrnaeans, Trallians, and his personal letter to Polycarp.

[2] "Ye, therefore, as well as all your fellow-travelers, are God-bearers, temple-bearers, Christ-bearers, bearers of holiness, adorned in all respects with the commandments of Jesus Christ, in whom also I exult that I have been thought

both body and spirit.[3] I was amazed that there was no exhortation to seek material success. There was no plea to claim the right of prosperity and material wealth. In fact, in Polycarp's *Letter to the Philippians*, he warns against the love of material goods. He spoke of following the Lord's Commandments, putting on the armor of righteousness, and teaching others to do the same.[4]

As the two disciples had walked on the road to Emmaus with Jesus and their hearts began to burn, my heart also began to burn. This was the Christianity I knew was revealed in the Gospels—Gospels that did not officially become part of the canon of Scripture until more than two hundred years after these men lived. I realized that this was the Christianity of the New Testament manifest in these men. These were holy men. These were men who knew the apostles. And it was this emphasis on personal holiness and the

---

worthy, by means of this Epistle, to converse and rejoice with you, because with respect to your Christian life ye love nothing but God only" (Ignatius' *Letter to the Ephesians*, chap. 9). *The Early Church Fathers* from the original 38 volumes by Harmony Media, Inc. Salem, Ore.: Harmony Media, © 2000.

[3] "Let us seek to be followers of the Lord (who ever more unjustly treated, more destitute, more condemned?), that so no plant of the devil may be found in you, but ye may remain in all holiness and sobriety in Jesus Christ, both with respect to the flesh and spirit" (ibid., chap. 10).

[4] "'But the beginning of all evil is the love of money.' Knowing therefore that 'we brought nothing into the world and we can take nothing out of it,' let us arm ourselves with the armour of righteousness, and let us first of all teach ourselves to walk in the commandment of the Lord; next teach our wives to remain in the faith given to them, and in love and purity, tenderly loving their husbands in all truth, and loving all others equally in all chastity, and to educate their children in the fear of God. Let us teach the widows to be discreet in the faith of the Lord, praying ceaselessly for all men, being far from all slander, evil speaking, false witness, love of money, and all evil, knowing that they are the altar of God, and that all offerings are tested, and that nothing escapes him of reasonings or thoughts, or of 'the secret things of the heart.'" (Polycarp's *Letter to the Philippians*, chap. 4:1–3).

Christian's influence in the world that drew me into a more serious reading of the early Church Fathers. After twenty years of teaching against modern Christian materialism, I finally felt vindicated. There, before me, I had the faith of the apostles as it had been handed to the next generation of apostolic Fathers, and this apostolic Christianity did not define itself in terms of material prosperity or embrace a "Christ-for-cash" Gospel.

As I read the historical background of Ignatius, I realized that he was indeed the second from Peter as bishop of the Church at Antioch, Euodius being the first. He knew John and the apostles. Here was a man who had known the apostles! In the back of my mind, a memory emerged of a time, about five years previously, when I heard Karl Keating, a seasoned Catholic apologist, in a debate with Dave Hunt (known for his strong anti-Catholic sentiments). Karl ended the debate by asking Dave, "Who would you believe to relay the details of an event accurately—an eyewitness—or someone who came along fifteen hundred years later and told you what he thought had happened?" At the time Karl said that, it made sense, but it was irrelevant to me because I couldn't relate to it. I thought it was a good point though, and it was the only point he made that night that had stuck with me all these years.

And now I could see it clearly. Karl Keating's point was suddenly very relevant. This truly was the Christianity of the apostles, told by the eyewitnesses. What touched me in particular was that I began to see it all unfold before me—this Christianity as it really is. When I read Ignatius, there it was! I saw this Christianity of the Gospels—a Christianity of sacrifice, a Christianity of love of Christ to the extent of leaving things that are good and legitimate just for love of him. This was Christianity! I could feel the holiness of

Ignatius and his passion and love for Christ emerging. And I could identify with his desire for the ultimate sacrifice, to die for the love of God.[5]

Ignatius of Antioch wanted to be a pure loaf for Christ, ground by the jaws of the wild beasts. I thought, "This is the heart and soul of Christianity—experiencing the transforming love of God and offering ourselves selflessly to God!" I understood his desire to be the wheat of God ground in the teeth of the lions. I said, *Yes! This is what it is all about! It is not about being healthy, wealthy, and wise; it's about what I can do to please God; what I can do to bring glory to God.* In reading these early Church documents, I had discovered apostolic Christianity in its original form, but I also discovered some things about the Christian faith that were not a part of my theology.

The Liturgy of the Church

First, I discovered that the early Church's worship was both charismatic *and* liturgical. By the time of Ignatius, the liturgical aspect of the Church was in ascendancy, and the charismatic aspect was subordinate to it. In the *Didache*,[6] I not only read about apostles and prophets and their roles in the

---

[5] "I write to all the churches, and I bid all men know, that of my own free will I die for God, unless ye should hinder me. I exhort you, be ye not an unseasonable kindness to me. Let me be given to the wild beasts, for through them I can attain unto God. I am God's wheat, and I am ground by the teeth of wild beasts that I may be found pure bread [of Christ]" (Ignatius' *Letter to the Romans* (Lightfoot's translation), chap. 4:1).

[6] The *Didache*, also called *The Teaching of the Twelve Apostles*, was an early Christian document used as a catechism to instruct neophytes entering the Church. It was found in a monastery in Constantinople in 1883. Although scholars differ on the date of its composition (A.D. 50 to A.D. 150), its internal material gives us a picture of primitive Christianity.

early Church,[7] but I also read about Christian worship that was liturgical.[8] The *Didache* spoke of a pure sacrifice,[9] prescribed prayers, and of Holy Communion as the Eucharist.[10]

Now my interest was really piqued, and I was flushed with the excitement of what I was discovering. I rummaged through my library and found an old book on the development of Christian worship that I had purchased years earlier at a garage sale, and I began to compare the information I was gleaning from the *Didache*. I was surprised at what I found. In my garage-sale book, Doctor Maxwell wrote about the first-century Christian worship service that included most everything in modern-day Catholic liturgy, *including* the "Celebration of the Lord's Supper, derived from the experience of the Upper Room". It was all there—right down to the "Kiss of Peace".[11]

[7] Ibid., chap. 11:1–21.
[8] Ibid., chaps. 9 and 10.
[9] Ibid., chap. 14:1, 4.
[10] Ibid., chap. 9:1.
[11] "Putting together, then, the references to worship in the New Testament in the light of later history—a reasonable course since the history is continuous—we arrive at something like this towards the end of the first century:

"First, that which grew out of the Synagogue: Scripture lections (1 Tim. iv:13; 1 Thes. v.27; Col. iv.16); Psalms and hymns (1 Cor. xiv.26; Eph. v.19; Col. iii.16); common prayers (Acts 2.42; 1 Tim. ii.1-2) and people's Amens (1 Cor xiv.16); a sermon or exposition (1 Cor. xiv.26; Acts xx.7); a confession of faith, not necessarily the formal recitation of a creed (1 Cor. xv.1-4; 1 Tim. vi.12); and perhaps almsgiving (1 Cor. xvi.1-2; 2 Cor. ix.10-13; Rom. xv.26).

"Secondly, commonly joined to the above, the Celebration of the Lord's Supper, derived from the experience of the Upper Room (1 Cor. x.16, xi.23; Matt. xxvi.26-8; Mark xiv.22-4; Luke xxii.19-20). The Prayer of Consecration would include thanksgiving . . . , remembrance of our Lord's death and resurrection . . . , intercession . . . , and perhaps the recitation of the Lord's Prayer. . . . Probably there were singings in this part of the service, and the Kiss of Peace. . . . The typical worship of the Church is to be found to this

Doctor Maxwell's description of early Christian worship provided significant insight into the transitional period of worship in the early Christian community. It was not difficult to see the formation of early Christian liturgy in the words and admonitions of Saint Paul in his letters to the Philippians (Phil 2:5–11) and to his "son" Timothy (1 Tim 2:1–2; 4:13). The fact became apparent that the fluidity of early Christian worship as recorded in the New Testament had, by the beginning of the second century, coalesced into a standard liturgy consisting of the public reading from the Old Testament Scriptures, Psalms, and "Memoirs of the Apostles" (the four Gospels), the admonitions from the bishop, the public prayers of intercession, the eucharistic prayers of Consecration, and the taking of an offering for the poor.

Here, I learned that by the opening years of the second century the governments of individual churches were tied together through a common apostolic tradition and organized around the hierarchical model of bishop, presbyter (priest, elder, or pastor), and deacon. I was surprised to learn that it is historically possible to trace the development of the Christian faith from many of the twelve apostles to Christianity today. After Saint James the Just was martyred at Jerusalem in 62, Jesus' relatives became bishops in Jerusalem until late in the second century (Eusebius, bk. 3). Saint Mark established Christianity in Egypt; Saint Thomas in India; Saint Andrew in Byzantium, later renamed Constantinople; Saint John in Ephesus; and Saint Peter in both

---

day in the union of the worship of the Synagogue and the sacramental experience of the Upper Room; and that union dates from New Testament times" (William D. Maxwell, B.B., Ph.D. *An Outline of Christian Worship* [London: Oxford University Press, 1936], pp. 4–5).

Antioch and Rome.[12] In his treatise against the second-century Gnostic Valentinus, Saint Irenaeus wrote about the universal Church. Even though it had spread throughout the world by his time, "the authority of the tradition is one and the same."[13] He further clarified that this was the Church handed down by the apostles and their successors to the present time. This was the Church that held the tradition of the faith and was founded in Rome by Saints Peter and Paul.[14]

There it was! The light of discovery was gleaming brightly for me now. Christianity had not apostatized from apostolic teaching nor had it dropped off the edge of the world. The message of the Cross had not been lost in Hellenistic philosophy or in the perversion of sub-apostolic Christians. By the opening of the second century, the *episkopoi*,

---

[12] *The Ecclesiastical History of Eusebius Pamphilus* (Grand Rapids: Baker Book House, 1995), p. 479.

[13] "The Church, after received this preaching and this faith, although she is disseminated throughout the whole world, yet guarded it, as if she occupied but one house.... For, while the languages of the world are diverse, nevertheless, the authority of the tradition is one and the same" (Irenaeus' "Against Heresies", in William A. Jurgens, *Faith of the Early Church Fathers*, vol. I [Collegeville, Minn.: Liturgical Press, 1970], p. 85).

[14] "And we are in a position to enumerate those who were instituted bishops by the Apostles, and their successors to our own times.... But since it would be too long to enumerate in such a volume as this the successions of all the Churches, we shall confound all those who, in whatever manner, whether through self-satisfaction or vainglory, or through blindness and wicked opinion, assemble other than where it is proper, by pointing out here the successions of the bishops of the greatest and most ancient Church known to all, founded and organized at Rome by the two most glorious Apostles, Peter and Paul. That Church which has the tradition and the faith which comes down to us after having been announced to men by the Apostles. For with this Church, because of its superior origin, all Churches must agree, that is, all the faithful in the whole world; and it is in her that the faithful everywhere have maintained the Apostolic tradition" (ibid., p. 90).

presbyteroi, and *diakonoi*[15] had evolved into the three-tier leadership found in the letters of Saint Ignatius of Antioch. It was these bishops, grounded in apostolic tradition, who guided and protected the second-century Church from the many heresies that cropped up in this critical period of Church history. Saint Ignatius admonished that nothing should be done without the approval and the authority of the bishop and urged being subject to the priests who represented the apostles. The deacons were there to serve as ministers of the church.[16] Working through and with this established hierarchy, he explained, is to be in harmony with God.[17] Indeed, we are to follow the lead of the bishops just as Jesus Christ follows God the Father. Wherever Jesus Christ is, there is the Catholic Church.[18]

---

[15] Greek for bishops, elders (priests), and deacons.

[16] "It is needful, then—and such is your practice—that you do nothing without your bishop; but be subject also to the presbytery as representing the Apostles of Jesus Christ, our hope, in whom we are expected to live forever. It is further necessary that the deacons, the dispensers of the mysteries of Jesus Christ, should win the approval of all in every way; for they are not dispensers of food and drink, but ministers of a church of God" (Ignatius' *Letter to the Trallians*, chap. 2).

[17] "I exhort you to strive to do all things in harmony with God: the bishop is to preside in the place of God, while the presbyters are to function as the council of the Apostles, and the deacons, who are most dear to me, are entrusted with the ministry of Jesus Christ" (Ignatius' *Letter to the Magnesians*, chap. 6).

[18] "See that ye all follow the bishop, even as Jesus Christ does the Father, and the presbytery as ye would the apostles; and reverence the deacons as being the institution of God. Let no man do anything connected with the Church without the bishop. Let that be deemed a proper Eucharist, which is [administered] either by the bishop, or by one to whom he has entrusted it. Wherever the bishop shall appear, there let the multitude [of the people] also be; even as, wherever Jesus Christ is, there is the Catholic Church" (Ignatius' *Letter to the Smyrnaeans*, chap. 8).

The Christian faith had logically and methodically developed into a collection of geographically separated churches with *one* common tradition (1 Cor 11:2; 2 Thess 2:15), rooted in apostolic teaching and leadership and authenticated through apostolic succession from the hands of the apostles themselves to the second-, third-, and fourth-generation bishops. It was plain and evident, and only the most obtuse and obstinate would deny it.

To my amazement, I also discovered that the Church has always been Eucharist-centered. In Luke's account of Saint Paul's visit to Troas,[19] the disciples gathered together on the first day of the week to "break bread", not to hear the great apostle preach. Acts 2:42 and 46–47, say the followers continued steadfastly in the apostles' teaching and doctrine and prayers, praise, and "breaking bread"! Oh, there it was again. Suddenly Saint Luke's recorded dialogue between the resurrected Christ and the two disciples on the Emmaus Road crystallized into an early Church's understanding that Jesus is recognized in "the breaking of bread", i.e., Holy Communion. Now a clearer picture of the early Church's view of the Lord's Supper began to emerge; it began to make sense—the early Church's worship centered on what the Church would later call the Eucharist,[20] but what we Protestants called Holy Communion. Saint Ignatius would write to the Ephesians: "Give ear to the bishop and to the presbytery with an undivided mind, breaking one Bread,

---

[19] Acts 20:7

[20] The Greek word, *eucharistia*, means thanksgiving. It first appeared in the writings of St. Ignatius of Antioch (107), St. Justin Martyr (148–55), and St. Irenaeus of Lyons (180–99). Seven other names for Eucharist are *Lord's Supper, Table of the Lord, the Lord's Body, the Holy of Holies*, to which may be added the following terms which vary from their original meaning: *Agape* (Love Feast), *Eulogia* (Blessing), and *Synaxis* (Assembly).

which is the medicine of immortality, the antidote against death, enabling us to live forever in Jesus Christ."[21]

And then there were the statements of Saint Ignatius, who *knew* Saint John the Apostle and *knew* what he taught, who in his writings spoke of the Eucharist, i.e., the "breaking of bread", as the Flesh of Jesus and the Blood of Jesus. I had believed that such teaching of transubstantiation[22] was an eleventh-century creation of the Catholic Church. But to my surprise, there it was in the writings of Saint Ignatius of Antioch, an apostolic disciple:

> I have no taste for corruptible food nor for the pleasures of this life. I desire the Bread of God, which is the Flesh of Jesus Christ, who was of the seed of David; and for drink I desire His Blood, which is love incorruptible.[23]

> [Heretics] abstain from the Eucharist and from prayer, because they do not confess that the Eucharist is the Flesh of our Savior Jesus Christ, Flesh which suffered for our sins and which the Father, in His goodness, raised up again.[24]

> Take care, then, to use one Eucharist, so that whatever you do, you do according to God: for there is one Flesh of our Lord Jesus Christ, and one cup in the union of His Blood;

[21] *Letter to the Ephesians*, chap. 20.

[22] The definition of *transubstantiation* is the complete conversion of bread and wine into the Body and Blood of Jesus, whereby he is truly and sacramentally present. Although the bread and wine maintain their physical appearances (accidents), they have *substantially* become Jesus' Flesh and Blood through the calling down of the Holy Spirit and the words of institution. Although the word *transubstantiation* was first used in the eleventh century, the concept of the Eucharist being changed into the Real Presence of Jesus Christ has been in the Church since apostolic times.

[23] *Letter to the Romans*, chap. 7.

[24] *Letter to the Smyrnaeans*, chap. 6.

one altar, as there is one bishop with the presbytery and my
fellow servants, the deacons.[25]

Writing sixty years later, Saint Justin Martyr confirmed the
Real Presence of Jesus Christ in the Eucharist:

And this food is called among us Eukaristia [the Eucharist],
of which no one is allowed to partake but the man who
believes that the things which we teach are true, and who
has been washed with the washing that is for the remission
of sins, and unto regeneration, and who is so living as Christ
has enjoined. For not as common bread and common drink
do we receive these; but in like manner as Jesus Christ our
Saviour, having been made flesh by the Word of God, had
both flesh and blood for our salvation, so likewise have we
been taught that the food which is blessed by the prayer of
His word, and from which our blood and flesh by trans-
mutation are nourished, is the flesh and blood of that Jesus
who was made flesh.[26]

Saint Irenaeus wrote in A.D. 199:

When, therefore, the mixed cup and the baked bread receives
the Word of God and becomes the Eucharist, the Body of
Christ, and from these the substance of our flesh is increased
and supported, how can they say that the flesh is not capable of receiving the gift of God, which is eternal life—flesh
which is nourished by the Body and Blood of the Lord,
and is in fact a member of Him?[27]

Now these men were careful to let us know that they could
not command as did the apostles, for they were not the
initiators—but the preservers of what they had received from

[25] *Letter to the Philadelphians*, chap. 3.
[26] *First Apology* 66.
[27] *Adversus Harereses, V*, 2.

the apostles (Jude 3). Saint Irenaeus wrote: "The preaching of the Church truly continues without change and is everywhere the same, and has the testimony of the Prophets and the Apostles and all their disciples. . . . That in which we have faith is a firm system directed to the salvation of men; and, since it has been received by the Church, *we guard it.*" [28]

I had made an astounding discovery here. I had found the pearl of great price—the true Christian faith in its essence, in its purity—flowing from the fountainhead. Three things began to emerge: (1) the early Church was liturgical as well as charismatic; (2) the Church had an established hierarchy by the opening of the second century; and (3) the center of Christian worship was and always has been Eucharist-centered. I saw emerging a picture of Christianity, of which I realized I had a variant form—powerful and effective, but nevertheless an incomplete form of the Christianity that flowed from the Upper Room.

Everything else was subordinate now—what I had believed, what I had been taught—all of it receded into its proper perspective. How had we missed all this? This was a rude awakening, and I felt naked. I felt unconnected to apostolic Christianity. I knew the faith I had was great because it worked, and I never doubted that God was with us. But the faith into which I was born was not exactly the same as the faith that history revealed to have flowed from apostolic times.

Still, I was not upset. I was excited because I was on a journey to find out as much about God as I could. It gave me a hunger to know more. The joy of discovery was unexplainable! I had discovered the Christian faith in its purest essence. Being Catholic still wasn't even on the radar screen at this point. That didn't even enter my mind. I was

<hr/>

[28] Ibid., Book III, 24 (italics added).

consumed with the fact that I had been correct about the Gospel message being one of servitude and sacrifice, not of ruling and indulgence.

Christian Worship as Sacrifice

Then in 1 Corinthians 10:21b, I read Paul saying, "You cannot partake of the table of the Lord and the table of demons." The word *table* is a synonym for altar. So Paul is saying we eat at the altar. Well, the altar, from my perspective as a Christian, was Calvary where Christ was offered. Then, what really intrigued me was what I read in the *Didache*[29]—when its author cautions, "So that your sacrifice might be pure, confess your sins"—okay, we've got a little confession going on there. But what is this sacrifice? Is it the sacrifice of your life? Is it the sacrifice of praise or of worship? What sacrifice is he talking about? There was a reference to Malachi 1:11, so I turned there, and it said, "For from the rising of the sun to its setting my name is great among the nations, and in every place incense is offered to my name, and a pure offering; for my name is great among the nations, says the LORD of hosts."

Now how could this pure sacrifice be offered all over the world? Paul was talking about the table of the Lord, and if the altar of the Lord is present within the Christian community, then that means there must be sacrifice—you don't have an altar without sacrifice. It was slowly beginning to come together. Well, I thought, Jerusalem is the place sacrifice is to be made. What kind of a sacrifice is going to be made all over the world? Ignatius answered that for me. He said, the Body and the Blood of our Lord.

---

[29] *Didache*, chap. 14.

And then I began to understand what Eucharist is—that it is not a symbol—it *is* the sacrifice of our Lord. So I reread John 6 and 1 Corinthians 11, and it started to become clear. When I read Justin Martyr saying, "We have received this from the apostles that it is not common bread and not common wine, but it has been changed into the Flesh of our Lord and the Blood of our Lord" [30] my eyes were opened. I saw clearly.

It arrested my attention because now I saw Christianity as it really was intended to be—from the source. The Eucharist is a sacrifice. It is truly the Blood of our Lord, and it is the Body of our Lord. All of the Church Fathers testified to it. Now rereading the Scriptures, it only made sense. "Jesus said to them, 'Truly, truly, I say to you, unless you eat the flesh of the Son of man and drink his blood, you have no life in you; he who eats my flesh and drinks my blood has eternal life, and I will raise him up at the last day'" (Jn 6: 53–54).

Now how could one man give the entire world his Flesh and his Blood? He could do it through the bread and the wine. A sacrifice in the Old Testament was never called pure. It was called clean, but never pure. This one was called pure. Oh, but it's he—the Lamb of God who takes away the sins of the world! Now I really was hooked. I saw that this was it! This was the truth! This was Christianity! But I was still not thinking as a Catholic.

Apostolic Tradition

It was the holy attitude of Ignatius of Antioch that started the ball rolling. Then, in reading Irenaeus, I kept reading

[30] *First Apology* 66.

the word *tradition*, and as I read what he kept saying about tradition and against heresies, it suddenly came to me that this all makes sense. They used this faith to fight heresies. That's how they were able to determine what a heresy was. The faith had been handed down from the apostles into what was now around the fourth generation, and they still measured themselves by the traditions they had received from the apostles.

A picture began to emerge as I read. I could see that the Church has always relied on tradition as well as Sacred Scripture. It is not something the Catholic Church invented. As I continued to read, Clement of Rome spoke of offering sacrifice and about ministers that offer sacrifice. Then I saw apostolic tradition in the context of the Church. It definitely wasn't something that was added on later. It has always been the context in which Sacred Scripture was placed. And that made it all the more meaningful and relevant. You judge what Scripture means by looking at it in its context—how it has traditionally been interpreted.

Baptismal Regeneration

That caused me to take another look at baptism. Oh, Christ really *did* mean water! That's ingenious! All of the Fathers say that we are born again through water and the Holy Spirit. Baptism, in the Pentecostal faith, was the confirmation of what you had already done in your heart. In Anabaptist theology, typical of most Protestant denominations—including Pentecostal and Baptist Evangelical—you have to make a decision before you can be baptized. Any baptism before the decision has been made is not considered a valid baptism because you have to believe and profess that belief first. But now I realized that the Church never taught that.

The Church taught that baptism, through the waters of regeneration, was the gateway to the Body of Christ. Justin Martyr said, "This we received from the apostles."

I read that Ignatius called the faith Catholic, but I recognized that he was describing it in its universal aspect. All I knew was that I had discovered the Church of Christ; that it didn't become corrupt as we had believed; that it didn't go under when the apostles died; that it had actually survived and grown!

And so, from the holiness and sacrificial love of Ignatius of Antioch to the penance of the Shepherd of Hermes in the confession of sins to the sacrifice of the *Didache* to the tradition of Irenaeus, who clarifies what that sacrifice is, I felt I had a pretty good idea of what Christian worship really was. It was much different than what I had thought. It was liturgical; it was hierarchical; and it was Eucharist-centered. This is the Church. We had put the emphasis on the gifts of the Spirit, on preaching. The emphasis was to be on neither of those, but rather, the emphasis was to be on Christ. *He* is the sacrifice.

It was time to introduce all my discoveries to my Wednesday night Bible study class.

8

The Truth

When Wednesday evening, March 18, 1998, arrived, I decided I needed to make some prior rearrangements of the worship space at Maranatha. I moved the altar to the center and took the presider's chair and the presbyter's chair and put them on the side, close to the altar. I had never set foot inside a Catholic Church during Mass, so I wasn't even thinking of imitating Catholicism. I was simply following what I had read was tradition in the Church.

I planned to follow the mode of worship from the *Apology* of Justin Martyr, in which he describes a Sunday morning worship experience.[1] I even separated the men from the women. I took some prayers from the *Didache* and blended them with some of the prayers from Justin Martyr so that we would have a eucharistic prayer, and I decided we would do just what they did in the early Church. I served communion, and many of the people came up to receive it, but some refused to come. My own mother wouldn't come forward. She told me, "I don't want no cookie!"

Overall, I would say the whole evening didn't go over very well. I thought to myself, "Now that that lesson is over, where do I go from here?" What was I going to do with this amazing knowledge I had just acquired? I knew I had found authentic Christianity. I couldn't just blow it away and say, "Okay, that was a great discovery, but I'm done

---

[1] Justin Martyr's *First Apology*, 67.

with it." This newfound knowledge had a tremendous impact
on me, and the greatest challenge, as I saw it, was, What
am I going to do now?

One thing I was sure of was that I needed help. I needed
some professional instruction concerning this material I was
reading that had touched my life so profoundly and had
changed me forever. I had utilized the extensive library at
Sacred Heart Major Seminary in Detroit on numerous occasions in the past. In fact, I began visiting there during the
mid- to late sixties. So I decided the seminary, with its
learned instructors, was a good place to start. I knew that it
was a Catholic school, and I was hopeful that someone there
taught about the Church Fathers and could help me. I made
a telephone call and was put in touch with theology professor Bill Riordan. I explained to him that I had uncovered a great treasure in the Church Fathers, I had discovered
the truest form of Christianity, and I was intrigued by it. I
explained that I now was at the point where I needed direction in my reading and gathering of facts. He first recom-
mended a four-volume set of books on patrology by Johannes
Quasten. He said it was the best you could get, and I thanked
him. He continued graciously to recommend the materials
I needed as I progressed in my study.

And the more I studied, the more confirmed I became
in this knowledge that what I had created within our own
church was an aberrant form of Christianity. I saw that many
Protestants had missed the mark. I recognized they had missed
the mark in the Eucharist. They had missed the mark in
the hierarchy of the Church. They had missed the mark
in the liturgy. It was puzzling to me. How could these men,
who were so smart and so well educated, miss this? How
could they miss it when a simple pastor like me could read
the early Church Fathers and figure it out?

I continued reading the early Church Fathers and the lives of the saints. Of particular interest to me was Saint Anthony of Egypt. I read of his sacrifice—giving away all his great family wealth and going into the desert. I had an affinity for him because I recognized how he could do that and why he did that. I realized that I too could have done that had I been in his place. I understood his thinking. (I would later choose Saint Anthony of Egypt as my patron saint.) Reading the lives of the early saints was like food to a starving soul. Reading the history of the Church and how it struggled for its existence, how it suffered, how it withstood heresy, confirmed all the more my belief that this was the true Christianity. Still, I had no thought of becoming Catholic.

But I knew I could not just continue in the tradition of Christianity I had received. I could not because now I saw it as an empty shell. It had been emptied of its relevance. It had been a good, but incomplete, tradition, which had served its purpose, but I had outgrown it. I now saw Christianity in a clearer light, a better light. How could I possibly live in its shadow? How could I go back and do what I'd always done now that I had seen Christianity in a purer light?

So I began to make changes—small changes that I thought my congregation could live with and wouldn't cause them to walk away. My idea was to bring apostolic Christianity into my church because this was the way the Church had always worshipped.

One change was that I began thinking more liturgically. Around Easter, I divided our service into the liturgy of the Word and the liturgy of the Eucharist. We were still having communion just once a month; I began offering it every Sunday. That was a stretch. One of my longtime congregants walked up to me and said, "Pastor, we used to have communion twice a year. Then, when we came to Maranatha, we had it once a month. Now we are having it every Sunday. Why are you doing all this changing?"

I told her, "This is the way the Church has always done it. This is Christian worship—centering the worship around the Eucharist."

I put candles on the altar to make it a more sacred setting. One of my parishioners said, "There you go with that Catholic stuff again."

I answered him, "Yeah, wait until next year, and I'll put Mary's picture on the wall!" I was being facetious, but no one laughed.

Slowly, as I continued to read, I became more excited because I could see that I was right on track. I made my own prayers, taking them from the Church Fathers and putting them together. I just wanted to be apostolic—to be as the Church had always been.

The people of my congregation had concerns, but they loved me and trusted me. They would say, "Pastor, you're becoming Catholic aren't you?"

I would say, "Good God, no! Why would I want to be Catholic?" I still had no intention of becoming Catholic. I loved the Word of God! I loved teaching the Bible! Why would I want to go back under those antiquated rules and regulations? Why would I want to put myself under that old historical monstrosity?

To me the Catholic Church was just an old institution— like an old man walking down the road, a person who had lost all of his vim and vigor—something that reminded one of the past. It had nothing redeemable in it, except perhaps memories.

I continued to implement changes, and my people were going through all kinds of changes and concerns of their own. Many thought I was being deceitful, but I really wasn't. I believed I was just putting our church back the way it was supposed to be. I could see clearly how we had created our own type of Christianity, and I knew that it wasn't the type of Christianity that had grown out of the apostles. All I wanted to do was to put our church back where it belonged.

I gradually became aware that maybe the Catholic Church might have something. Perhaps it was because, in all of my readings of the Church Fathers, they would keep using the word *Catholic*. Catholic, Catholic, Catholic—and, of course, I knew the Catholic Church was an established entity. Although I had no desire to become Catholic, I thought perhaps I could see what they were doing, and I could pick up some things from them since the Church had been called Catholic all the way back to Ignatius.

A couple of months after our first early Christian worship service; I was flipping through the television channels and happened on the Eternal Word Television Network (EWTN) while they were televising a Catholic Mass. I recognized it and watched with great interest and thought, "Now that's Christian worship." As I watched I saw all the elements of what Justin Martyr had spelled out, and I understood what they were doing.

It was about that time that Professor Riordan asked me to meet him for lunch at a local sub shop. As we ate, I enthused about my growing knowledge of the early Church and my discovery that it was Eucharist-centered and that the Eucharist was truly the Blood of Christ and the Flesh of Christ. A very knowledgeable, kind, and soft-spoken man, Professor Riordan smiled at my enthusiasm and asked if I had ever attended a Catholic Mass. Of course I hadn't, but I jumped at his invitation to join him for a weekday service.

The first Catholic Mass I attended was at Saint Fabian in Farmington Hills. I walked in and thought, "Wow, this is how it is done." I was transfixed. I could see all the elements I had learned and read about—and were millennia old—in operation. It was awesome!

Doctor Riordan took me to the tabernacle and told me, "Jesus is in there. I thought you might want to pause a moment and pray." And I understood because I had read in the early Church Fathers that once the bread was consecrated, it remained consecrated.

I was more determined than ever to continue implementing changes at Maranatha. I had bought vestments some time ago, shortly after we started Maranatha, for my niece's wedding. I wore a chasuble and an alb then too, but it was just a one-time thing, and I hung them back up after the service where they collected dust over the ensuing years. So I dusted off the robe and the alb and began wearing them again, and it made people very uncomfortable and nervous.

In our deacons' meetings, they would ask, "Pastor, what are you doing?"

I answered, "I'm being apostolic!"

One of the deacons commented that it was good to know those things for historical purposes, but wanted to know why we were incorporating them into worship.

I said, "Well, this is Christianity. This is the way it has always been."

He essentially told me, "Well, that's not what we have known, and we don't want to know it now!" They were definitely uncomfortable with it.

I bought a linen cloth for the altar and took the Bible off. And, of course, there were the candles. That was really being Catholic.

I actually went to a Catholic bookstore and bought a lectionary and figured out the cycles. I told my four ordained elders that when I was not there they were always to confine their preaching to the readings of the day. Well, you never tell Pentecostals how to preach! The Spirit leads one in what to preach. They were indignant about that. They said, you don't tell us how to preach! The Holy Ghost tells us how to preach!

What finally drove them away was the Eucharist—saying it was the body and blood of Jesus. That and the fact that I was now teaching regenerational baptism was just too much for many of them. As Evangelicals and Pentecostals, we just didn't believe that. It was not a sacrament; it was an ordinance. It was something you did as a law of the Church. There was no saving grace. The Lord's Supper was merely a memorial feast. Baptism was simply recognition that one has received genuine faith and has been included in the Christian community. It was a sign of a spiritual baptism.

So when I uncovered the Fathers' teachings that baptism with water was indeed the new birth—and that is all through the Fathers' writings and in the Bible—I preached that. My nephew, who was one of my ordained elders, came into my office even before I could take my vestments off, and he was hot! Another elder—a good man and a good friend—came in, and he was visibly upset.

My nephew asked, "Do you actually believe that we are born again through water baptism?"

I said, "Yes, I just preached that."

He said, "I don't believe that."

The other elder said, "I know that isn't right because I got baptized as a Baptist and I went down a dry devil and came up a wet devil—I didn't get nothin'! I went back and picked up my pack of Kools and started smoking just like I always did. I didn't get nothin' until I got the baptism of the Holy Spirit."

I said, "Now listen, when you were baptized, were you baptized with the intention of being a child of God?"

He said, "Absolutely!"

I said, "Well, your problem was that you didn't continue. It wasn't that the baptism wasn't efficacious. You just didn't continue."

He would hear none of that and said, "No, man, the only thing that stopped me from sinning was the baptism of the Holy Spirit." He walked away.

My nephew walked away.

I began to use real wine—we had always used grape juice in the past—and my people wouldn't drink it.

Another elder said, "I don't believe that the bread and the wine are really the Body and Blood of Christ."

I said, "It's in the Bible. It is in Church teaching."

He said, "I still don't believe it." He left to look for another church home.

As my congregation began to fall apart, everything began to come together for me. I eventually began to wonder by whose authority did men like Martin Luther and Calvin bring change into the Church that had been teaching consistently for fifteen centuries. Martin Luther was a monk, not a bishop. Calvin wasn't even a priest! And yet they tried to bring novel doctrines into the Church. And then I understood that there had been some tinkering with the faith by these men!

I got really excited! What else had I missed? I read the *Shepherd of Hermas* and saw how penance was defined by the Church. All of these things had been in the Church in seed form. As the Church grew in understanding itself, these seeds began to blossom.

We Protestants said, well, that was added later. But no, it wasn't added—it had been there from the beginning. The seeds were there in the teachings of Jesus. The seeds were there in Scripture. Most important, the seeds were there in apostolic tradition, as something handed down from the first to the second to the third to the fourth generation. It had always been there.

The same applied to the teachings about Mary. They were always there, but were latent teachings that came out only after the Church struggled with heresy. Who was Jesus of Nazareth? Was he divine or wasn't he? He was born of a woman, but who was this woman? Was she the mother of Jesus or the mother of Christ, or the mother of God?

The Church had to handle this problem. It determined that Mary is the Mother of God because Jesus is God. I began to understand that the Church passed on this faith from one generation to the next, and, as each generation received it, they had to use it to address their particular generation and the heresies that cropped up in that generation. And what they used as a defense was, "We received this from the apostles." They were faithful to the tradition handed down from the apostles.

Then I read 2 Thessalonians 2:15; Paul tells his followers to be careful to observe all the *paradosis* he had delivered to them. And the word *paradosis* means traditions. Whether written (as in the Bible) or oral.

Well, that knocked *Sola Scriptura* (the "Bible alone" theology) right out of the water. The Church has never ever adopted the position that the Bible is our *only* teaching authority. That's why we realize that Martin Luther didn't attempt to reform the Church; he reinterpreted it. He tried to make changes without authority and didn't go back to the beginning, to *what was handed down from the apostles*.

In the early days of the Church, Christians weren't running around with Bibles in their hands. All that were available were the Old Testament Scriptures and very few of those. Plus, most people couldn't read anyway. The teachings of the Old Testament had already been interpreted by Jesus and the apostles, and those teachings were handed down orally. The Christian faith was handed down through the traditions of the Church. This only made sense.

There were some elements within the Christian faith that were latent in Scripture—that were not brought forth until there was need for definition and explanation. The seven sacraments were instituted by Christ, and I could see that, but they were in seed form. As the Church grew and had to define itself, so grew also these teachings of the Church. They were not novel teachings that were added on. They had always been there. I began to realize that it was the Catholic Church that gave the world Christianity—period! She is the mother of the Christian faith.

By the end of 1998, I had come to understand that the Catholic Church was, indeed, the Church of Jesus Christ. The traditions of the Church were authentic. This was how the Church had evolved, not the way we thought it had evolved. I decided we needed to identify with the Church, but I thought we could do that without becoming a part of the Catholic Church. I wanted to replicate it. I wanted to become *like* them, not *be* them. Heck, I didn't want to just throw my church away! Although I knew this was authentic Christian worship, I decided I didn't need to be Catholic in order to worship that way.

I made plans for 1999 to celebrate Epiphany, the Lenten season, the Easter season, and All Saints Day wearing the colors associated with the liturgical seasons. In my book of plans for the coming year I wrote:

> Our goal is to merge African-American charismatic tradition with ancient apostolic tradition. This merger will result in a unique blend of traditional Christian worship with an African-American contemporaneous flair, African-American charismatic worshipping in apostolic tradition. This new direction is a challenge calling for reexamination of our philosophy of worship, learning new and unfamiliar music and practicing the historical rites of liturgical worship.
>
> Our past experience has been unrehearsed and extemporaneous. It was a worship of the soul—spontaneous and emotional. As we grow into a unique form of worship, we must now become familiar with ancient responses, antiphons, litanies, and anthems. Our spirituality is not diminished nor is our love for Christ sacrificed by our new growth, but enhanced and enlarged as we draw near to God with reverence and divine order.
>
> The symbols and rites of apostolic tradition are not dead traditions or empty acts of worship, but visible expressions of our love for Christ and his work of redemption. Of all people we who have shared in the Pentecostal and charismatic experience can really appreciate the sacredness and reverence that apostolic tradition brings to our faith. What is new to us is really centuries old. Our new approach to Christian worship is a step back in time.
>
> What we are seeking is historical and spiritual continuity with the Church of the apostles, prophets, martyrs, fathers, and the saints of old. They all worshipped in established liturgical practices, which come down to us today in the Catholic, Orthodox, Lutheran, Anglican, Coptic, and Episcopal churches. What Protestants call Catholic-style worship is historical Christian worship. Many of the newer forms of worship are really deviations from established Christian worship.

Now that we worship God according to apostolic tradition we have become one with Christ's universal church
that covers all of the earth with 2,000 years of sacred history.

I was satisfied with my plan of action until one of the
brothers of my congregation asked me, "Pastor, what are
we? Are we Catholic or Protestant?"

That really started me thinking. I had to answer him honestly. "I don't know", I said.

"Well then," he continued, "what will I tell my children
that we are?"

I just wasn't willing to take that step. I knew I wasn't
Protestant. I could never be Protestant again because I understood what the Protestant church had done. They had broken with tradition, and you can't break with tradition and
continue with all that Christ wanted you to have.

So that was a painful moment for me. I had to decide
what we were going to do. In all my enthusiasm to become
apostolic and rediscover the Church, I came to the realization that I was recreating the wheel.

Why was I doing this? If this has already been done by
the Church that was authorized to do it, why was I trying
to redo it? Could that mean that I *should* be a part of that
Church? Why should I recreate what has already been tried,
proven true, practiced and refined?

I began to realize that I was becoming Catholic without
knowing it. That brother's questions had started me thinking, and I knew I had to make some very difficult decisions. I was out there all alone mimicking an institution
that already existed.

What finally convinced me to become Catholic was, in
the course of my studies, discovering two things that opened
my eyes to the light. The first was the promise of Jesus to

Peter that the gates of hell would never prevail against the Church; the second was the promise of Jesus that the Holy Spirit would never leave the Church. Jesus promised that the Holy Spirit would lead us to all truth and would be with us forever. Now, if that was true, and that was what Jesus said, and Jesus is God the Son, then the Church that he inaugurated in the Upper Room was the Church to which he gave the gift of perpetuity and the gift of inviolability or incorruptibility. With these gifts, *the Church* was inaugurated in the Upper Room. There was no great falling away. The Church did not fall, did not fail, and did not apostatize. There was no corruption because hell could never overthrow it. Even through persecution exteriorly or interiorly, it could never be corrupted because the Holy Spirit is its soul. Now, all that I needed was to be certain I had found that Church which had started in the Upper Room!

Well, it couldn't be mine because I had started my church in 1982. It wasn't the Pentecostal church because that started in 1896. And it certainly wasn't the Baptist church that was started in 1612. I knew it couldn't be the Lutheran church because that was started in 1520. There could only be one.

Oh boy, I thought, *now how much are you really after the truth? If you acknowledge this truth, it could cost you everything you have ever loved and ever worked for. The Catholic Church is the Church of Jesus Christ. This is the Church that was inaugurated in the Upper Room. This is the Church that has the gifts of perpetuity and incorruptibility. This is the Church of Jesus Christ, and what it teaches is truth!*

Are you big enough to accept this? In accepting it you may lose everything! You may lose your family. You may lose your children and your wife. You may lose everything you hold dear! Now, what are you going to do?

It took me about a nanosecond to decide.

I said, "I have to acknowledge this. I *have* found the Pearl of Great Price! Though it may cost me everything, I know I have found the Church of Jesus Christ and, for this Church, no price is too high! For this Church, I am willing to give my life!"

For me, this was the fullness of revelation. I had found Christ in 1958, and now I had found his Church forty years later in 1998. I had the full picture. That picture was now complete, and I would die rather than to deny it.

I knew then that I would lose many of my people because they would never accept it. But I could not deny what I knew to be true.

I knew that I knew that I knew.

Photo 12. Mothers of the church at Maranatha in the late
1980s. Alex' mother, Margaret, is second from
the right. The mothers of the church were well-
respected for their knowledge of the faith.

Photo 13. Alex with his ministerial staff of Maranatha in the mid to late 1980s. Alex' cousin, Dave Winans, father of the gospel singing group, is on the left.

Photo 14. Alex, pastor of Maranatha in the mid to late 1980s.

Photo 15. Alex, pastor of Maranatha, around 1989.

Photo 16. Alex with the Maranatha choir in the early 1990s.

Photo 17. Donna's sister, Debbie Gillespie, with sons Matthew (left) and Jeremy around 1990.

Photo 18. Donna with her sister, Dianne, on June 5, 1993.

Photo 19. Alex, pastor of Maranatha, 1995.

9

What in Heaven's Name Am I Doing?

I knew by this time that I was Catholic in heart, mind, and soul. But I still had plenty of questions—questions that I had to come to terms with myself as well as for my congregation and, most especially, for my family. I began to formulate, in my own mind, the questions I knew would be asked of me.

Question 1: Why should we leave our faith if it worked for our parents and for us? We have found nothing wrong with our religious traditions. God has heard our prayers, saved us, comforted us, matured us spiritually, and brought us to where we are today. How can we deny what God has given to us? Why should we change to another religion that we don't know—one that is completely foreign to us?

This was the basic question I knew I had to answer. Our religious tradition was a blend of two powerful streams of faith: (1) African-American Christianity built on Protestant foundations, but unique in its spirituality, and (2) Pentecostalism, which was exceptionally amenable to a people who needed an energizing faith to face the suffering of social and racial disparities.

African-American spirituality is a "soulful" experience. It is rooted in a one-on-one relationship with God that is sensate—almost tangible. It can be felt and experienced. God is not known by theological reflection, but by an inner sense of his presence. One does not "learn" about God, one "experiences" God! As a consequence, African-American spirituality speaks of "feeling God", of being "touched by God", of "hearing God's voice". The soul's response to this God-soul union is a total surrendering of the self to the *Spirit*; hence, the highly emotive "letting go and letting God" outbursts so characteristic of African-American worship.

Added to this unique spirituality was our powerful Pentecostal faith, which was sort of a completion to our rich African-American heritage. Our propensity to relate to our Creator through the surrender of our inner selves proved to be fertile ground for the baptism of the Holy Spirit (Mt 3:11; Acts 1:8). Through this spiritual experience, the Holy Spirit sanctified our emotional responses to God and offered them up before the throne of grace as the legitimate outpourings of a deeply spiritual people (Rom 15:16). We not only enjoyed an intense spiritual experience with God, but now our offering up of faith was also enriched with spiritual gifts and spiritual knowledge. This combination of self-surrender with a powerful spiritual experience made our faith tradition complete and fulfilling.

So, how could I even dare to bring up the idea of embracing another faith tradition that was completely foreign to us and opposite to everything we considered spiritual? How could I make a centuries-old, ritualistic religion, steeped in philosophical and theological dogma and expressed in a subdued European spirituality that we considered *dead*, meaningful to my people? How could I possibly introduce liturgy and formal rites to a congregation whose entire ethos was deeply rooted in a personal and emotional approach to God?

How could I switch from, "Praise the Lord, everybody" to *"Dominus vobiscum"*?

From the beginning I had to recognize the legitimacy of our own faith tradition. I could not in good conscience demean or disparage who we were or what we had received of God. It was real. It worked for us. God was powerfully with us, and that was a fact that could not be denied. But we would not be *disowning* our spiritual heritage if we saw our faith as an indigenous response to faith and simply moved to broaden our spiritual experience by embracing Christianity in its universal and completed form. If we added to our African-American/Pentecostal heritage the historical Christian faith in its universal dimensions we would not be *abandoning* our faith, we would simply be *growing* in it. While it is true our paradigm would indeed have to shift in order to incorporate the full revelation of the Christian faith, we would continue to be "soulful", emotional, Holy-Ghost-filled, African-American Pentecostals who had simply embraced the Christian faith in its entirety.

Question 2: And if our faith is suddenly so inadequate and incomplete, why is it that our spirituality is far greater than those of the Catholic faith? We have progressed much further down the road of holiness than they have. Catholics smoke, drink, gamble, and generally live "loose lives". How can we be part of such a compromising faith? Won't we lose our testimony and distinctiveness as holiness *people? And why should we take on their religion if it has not produced a lifestyle of holiness equal to or greater than our own?*

This also was a difficult question to answer. As a Pentecostal, Holiness church we cut our spiritual teeth on two

Scriptures—Hebrews 12:14: "Strive for peace with all men, and for the holiness without which no one will see the Lord", and Acts 2:4: "And they were all filled with the Holy Spirit, and began to speak in other tongues, as the Spirit gave them utterance." We were taught that smoking, drinking, gambling, and all other "vices" were sinful and should be avoided. In fact, the more extreme holiness groups taught against Christmas trees, Easter, dancing, television, movies, plays, shorts, women's slacks, jewelry, and women's makeup. I grew to know that these things were not sinful, yet many I shepherded still viewed some of these activities as obstacles to spiritual maturity. The only answer I could give was that these prohibitions were the ingrained customs of our holiness *tradition* and not the belief of all Christians.

While it was true that many of my parishioners had attained a high degree of spirituality, it was pharisaical for them to look down their noses at those struggling to grow spiritually. This so-called "mark of distinction" was nothing more than spiritual arrogance. True spirituality is not found in the pride of spiritual accomplishment, but in the humble recognition that we are all sinners at various stages of growth and development. Such arrogance was the target of Jesus' parable of the self-righteous Pharisee who prided himself on not being like other men (Lk 18:13). We frequently boasted that our church was a hospital for sinners, a refuge for those who had lost their way, yet some found it so easy to condemn Catholics who had not reached their degree of spiritual maturity. As far as Catholicism not producing saints, I think history gives eloquent testimony to the tens of thousands of Catholics who have demonstrated their love of God through heroic holiness.

Question 3: We have begun in the Spirit (see Gal 3:3), so why are we now seeking to be perfected in the flesh (rituals, ceremonies, and man-made doctrines)? We've been taught all our lives that Catholics are unholy, insincere, worldly semi-pagans who hide behind weekly confession to a priest! Catholics are idol-worshipping, bead-rubbing, Mary-worshipping, superstitious people. They pray to saints, believe in Purgatory and that whatever the pope says is the truth. They burn candles and incense and pray to statues and icons and confess their sins to a man. All of our lives we have been taught that all of these things are superstition, idolatry, and man-made traditions! We've been taught that we can go directly to God without any human help, and we've developed a personal relationship with Christ. We don't need the intervention of Mary, the saints, or a priest!

First, this line of questioning not only demonstrated an ignorance of the teachings of the Catholic Church, but also underlined a deep-seated prejudice against Catholics. It reeks of four hundred years of bigotry and religious intolerance. The key words in this question were, *"we were taught"*. Yes, we were taught many negative things about what Catholics believe, and I discovered that all of them were perversions of what the Catholic Church really teaches. The Rosary, Marian veneration, the communion of saints, Purgatory, and the sacrament of reconciliation were not acts of superstition, but avenues of grace that God had so graciously made available to his beloved people. *We were taught* these things were superstitious acts, but in fact they were the pious acts of the people of God who sought to deepen their personal faith in the paschal mystery of Jesus Christ in whom we all are living members, both living and departed. Because it was not in *our* faith tradition we labeled it *superstition*.

Second, finding God or completing our salvation had absolutely nothing to do with our becoming Catholic. Our salvation became an accomplished fact the moment we made the fundamental option to serve Jesus Christ as our Savior and Lord. Although I never subscribed to the faith-alone teaching, I nevertheless believed, and still do, that our response to God and his response to us was both legitimate and complete (Col 2:10). What we didn't know was that liturgy and rituals had formed early in the Church's history. Rituals and sacred actions were symbols of eternal mysteries. Each movement expressed some spiritual proclamation that the Church held dear. The prayers of the Church were rooted in the Jewish daily prayers and offerings. The synagogue style of reading Sacred Scripture, prayers, hymns, and preaching became the form of worship Christians would later call the Liturgy of the Word. Even the love feast that figured so prominently in the apostolic church, but was later dropped from Christian worship in the sub-apostolic age, symbolized the "one bread" of the people of God. The Church has always used rituals, creeds, symbols, and icons to signify, clarify, and transmit the faith.

As far as confessing our sins to a priest, no other sacrament outside of baptism and the Eucharist, has a more biblical basis than that of the sacrament of reconciliation (confession). In his very first Resurrection appearance, Jesus gave the apostles his divine authority to pronounce the forgiveness of sins:

> On the evening of that day, the first day of the week, the doors being shut where the disciples were, for fear of the Jews, Jesus came and stood among them and said to them, "Peace be with you." ... Jesus said to them again, "Peace be with you. As the Father has sent me, even so I send you." And when he had said this, he breathed on them,

and said to them, "Receive the Holy Spirit. If you forgive the sins of any, they are forgiven; if you retain the sins of any, they are retained" (Jn 20:19, 21–23).

Thus Jesus gave to his apostles the same authority to forgive sins he himself had used in his earthly ministry, and it has caused the same adverse reaction today that it caused then (Mk 2:5–11). The same rebuttal is heard today: "It is blasphemy! Who can forgive sins but God alone?" (Mk 2:7). The answer is simple; a sovereign God can give whatever he wants to whomever he wills! The indisputable fact is, the Bible records Jesus giving the authority to forgive sins, i.e., to bind and loose (Mt 18:18), to his apostles. This "binding and loosing" authority was an inherent part of their governing authority and would be handed on to their successors, the bishops. The interpretation that the apostles fulfilled this text by proclaiming forgiveness through the preaching of the Gospel does not adequately explain the "retaining of sin" aspect of Jesus' words.

Karl Keating observes: "If God has already forgiven all a man's sins or will forgive them all, past and future, on a single act of repentance, then it makes little sense to tell the apostles they have been given the power to 'retain' sins, since forgiveness would be an all-or-nothing thing and nothing could be 'retained'." [1]

Granted, there was historical development in the application of the sacrament itself, yet the seeds for auricular confession were plainly laid in the words of Jesus himself.

Question 4: The Catholic Church doesn't even believe in the Bible, and most Catholics I know don't even know Jesus Christ

---

[1] Karl Keating, *Catholicism and Fundamentalism* (San Francisco: Ignatius Press, 1988), p. 185.

as their personal Lord and Savior! In fact, we know that Catholics are leaving their churches by the thousands. They come to Bible-believing churches, get saved, get filled with the Spirit, and begin to grow in the things of God.

Why, in heaven's name, should we go to an institution that is losing multitudes of people who constantly testify that they were not spiritually fulfilled or helped, but were bored to tears with dead liturgy—listening to a ten-minute homily by a dead, unspiritual, non–Holy Ghost priest—and lifeless rituals?

The two greatest slanders against Catholics are that they don't believe in the Bible and that they don't have a personal relationship with the Lord Jesus Christ. Catholics *do* believe in the Bible, and they *do* have a personal relationship with Jesus. As a matter of historical fact, the Catholic Church discerned the books that would comprise the Bible. One of the earliest determinations of a canon (the official catalog of divinely inspired writings, known as the Old and New Testaments) occurred around A.D. 360 at the Council of Laodicea with a list of books very similar to the modern-day canon. At the Council of Trent (1545 to 1563), the final determination of canonical books was defined. These seventy-two books, including the seven Old Testament deuterocanonical books rejected by the Reformation, were considered "sacred and canonical". The Catholic Church is the historical witness and the protector of revelation and is herself built upon Sacred Scriptures, Sacred Tradition, and the Magisterium. There is more Scripture reading in a Catholic Mass than there is in most Protestant churches on any given Sunday morning! The Catholic Church teaches that ignorance of Scripture is ignorance of Christ![2]

[2] Vatican Council II, *Dei Verbum*, no. 25.

One doesn't have to go far to find parishioners leaving a particular church. In fact, the word *church-hopper* originated in Protestant circles and is used to describe disgruntled church members who, with great regularity, move their membership from one church to another. And, what is the one reason church-hoppers give for moving from church to church? They're not being fed!

It is blatant religious prejudice to conclude that priests are unspiritual simply because they're Catholic. Yes, of course, there are priests who do things they shouldn't, but Catholics don't have a monopoly on unspiritual leadership. Failure in religious vocation is not an exclusively *Catholic* problem; it's a *human* problem to which all religions in all ages can attest. As is usually the case, we focus our attention on those who *fail* rather than those who quietly go about the work of the Lord with fear and trembling.

Question 5: How can we deny the moving and the gifts of the Holy Spirit and go sit in these dead, lifeless services that even the Catholics don't like? We love our lively worship and songs that we've grown up with! Why should we have to change to something so culturally foreign and unsatisfying? No offense to these White folks, but why do we need to become like them?

By far, this was the most difficult question, and it needed an in-depth answer. Spontaneity and freedom of expression are part and parcel of African-American religious heritage. We are free to express ourselves to what we perceived as the moving of the Holy Spirit. When we feel particularly touched by a song or testimony, we wave our hands or stand on our feet and demonstrate our agreement with what's being said or done. Our preachers don't simply *tell* us facts;

they *dialogue with us* as they paint a picture or tell the story. Those unfortunate ministers who cannot "tell the story" well are good "talkers", but the best they can glean from their audiences is an occasional "amen". The pulpiteers who can tell the story and awaken the imagination of their audience are highly prized gifts in the Black community. They invite their people to "walk with them" as they skillfully paint a picture so vivid in colors a blind man could distinguish the hues. It is utterly breathtaking to participate in a well-delivered Black sermon. In this, the heart and soul of African-American worship, the Holy Spirit skillfully unites the preacher, the musician, and the people into one harmonious *event* that not only speaks to the people, but also delivers them from their burdens and gives them hope and courage to survive another day. Black folk do not simply hear sermons—they feel them and enter into them! Gifted Black preachers bring their people into the message. They are made to feel like *they* are being called out of Egypt, *they* are in the boat on the stormy Galilee, and *they* are on the sidelines watching an outmatched David bring down an undefeated Goliath. Listening to such powerful sermons are spiritual experiences that make life both meaningful and bearable for thousands of African-Americans. That's why Black folk rate their worship services as either "good" or "so-so", depending on how they were ministered to by the entire worship experience. They talk about having *had* church as opposed to *attending* church. When they've *had* church, the Holy Spirit showed up and touched them; when they attended church, well, they just fulfilled a duty.

Another area that had to be addressed was the forfeiture of our music. It is most unfortunate that when some Whites comment on African-American religious music they disparagingly define it as "rock and roll". Such comments demonstrate a failure to grasp that in Black culture there is a consistent, fundamental beat that permeates all of our music, whether it's jazz, blues, pop, or gospel. This is *our* beat, it speaks to *us*, it touches *us*, it comforts *us*, and it is part of *our* group identity. Music without this beat can be great music, but it's not *our* music. This loud, rhythmic music plays a significant part in modern African-American worship. Long ago the old Negro spirituals gave way to gospel music. African-American congregations seldom, if ever, sing such traditional spirituals as *Swing Low, Sweet Chariot*—unless, of course, it's a special occasion—now they rock the house with *Jesus Is the Rock* or *Have You Tried My Jesus*. And, if we add the growing influence of Pentecostalism, today's African-American worship is more celebrative and Bible-oriented, with an emphasis on lifting up the name of Jesus, glorifying the Father, proclaiming the power of God's love, and extolling the delivering power of faith. No longer is heard the mournful songs that speak of suffering Black folk. Now, a whole new dimension of energetic praise and worship has blossomed in Black churches, transporting the hearer from the misfortunes and injustices of a hostile environment to the loving arms of a mighty God who can turn the darkness of adversity into the light of victory.

A still greater problem was how to deal with the loss of the operation of the charismatic gifts. The gifts of prophecy, tongues, healing, discernment, and word of knowledge were a basic and fundamental part of our theology and way of life; how could we simply walk away from these rich experiences and submit to a non-emotive, ritualistic liturgy? I understood clearly what many were saying, and I had to think it through to find a truthful response.

Faced with the daunting task of providing truthful answers to these difficult questions, I prayed and asked God for wisdom and guidance. He led me to do two things: first, teach the significance of the Mass; second, slowly lead my parishioners to experience the Mass within the context of our rich African-American heritage.

I had to begin with the concept of worship itself. Worship is the outpouring of the heart and spirit to God through forms, postures, gestures, and symbols determined worshipful by one's culture. We as African Americans have created a worship tradition drawn from our innate predispositions toward the divine, our spiritual experiences, our sufferings, and our interpretations of God's self-revelation to us as Black people. Although we are descendants of African slaves, we are not African. We have developed our own worship forms, music, perspectives, and responses to God that are uniquely *African-American*. As cited earlier, our worship tends to be celebrative, joyful, spontaneous, and free. But there are times when the joyful and celebrative must give way to the contemplative and reverential. The same God who said, "Make a joyful noise to the LORD" (Ps 100:1), also said, "The LORD is in his holy temple; let all the earth keep silence before him" (Hab 2:20). Yes, there are times of rejoicing and joyful praise, but there are other times when divine mysteries are present and demand reflection, silence, and awe. The beauty of the Latin Mass is that it can accommodate both joyful praise and deep spiritual reflection.

Throughout Church history the celebration of Eucharist has pride of place in Christian worship. As he is led step by step into the presence of the Lamb of God in his re-presentation on Calvary, the worshipper is reminded of the heavenly scene in the Book of Revelation (Rev 5). The broken, bleeding Lamb came forth from the throne of God, took the book of man's destiny and broke the seven seals, and with that action the entire universe, in awe, prostrated itself and cried, "Worthy ...". In like manner, when the priest places his hands over common bread and wine and calls down the power of the Holy Spirit to transubstantiate them into the Flesh of Jesus and the Blood of Jesus, we are called to be eyewitnesses to the greatest mystery in the universe. Through the eyes of faith, we see the Lamb of God made sacramentally present to us under the forms of Bread and Wine. God the Father is present, God the Son lays before us on the altar, and the Holy Spirit has manifested the greatest miracle of all. All of heaven, including angels, is present at the Lord's Table as Jesus gives us his Flesh to eat.

After spending weeks teaching on the sacrifice of the Mass, I slowly began to transform our Sunday worship service into a liturgical form of worship. Mindful of our joyful celebration, we kept our praise and worship songs but divided our worship into the liturgy of the Word and an approximation of the liturgy of the Eucharist. Each month I would add another element of the Roman Rite until, by the end of 1999, our Sunday worship was fully Catholic in appearance except, of course, for our praise and worship songs. And it worked! Slowly my people became attached to liturgical worship. They grew in their understanding and appreciation of the concept of sacrifice in worship.

But how would we deal with the loss of the gifts of the Spirit? The answer came in reading the lives of the saints. The charismatic gifts never ceased to operate within the Catholic Church. There has always been a charismatic dimension within the Church, but principally in the lives of the saints. Gregory Thaumaturgus (the Wonderworker), Moses the Black, Anthony of Padua, Father Solanus Casey, and Padre Pio were just a few of a long list of saints and holy people who possessed the charismatic gifts of miracles, healings, and bilocations. In fact, the Catholic Church has the largest number of charismatics of any Pentecostal/charismatic denomination: 75 to 100 million worldwide. Besides, there are times and opportunities for the operation of the gifts of the Spirit in prayer meetings, revivals, conferences, and in some cases, in charismatic Masses. In other words, our becoming Catholic would not be a denial of who we were; to the contrary, it would only be coming into full union with the one, holy, catholic, and apostolic New Testament Church.

Question 6: Will we still be able to fellowship with other non-Catholic churches?

Since the Second Vatican Council, the Catholic Church is far more open to and accepting of non-Catholic Christians. In fact, the Church recommends praying and working with other Christians in promoting unity and the common good. In the Second Vatican Council's decree on ecumenism, the Council Fathers observed: "In certain circumstances, such as in prayer services 'for unity' and during ecumenical gatherings, it is allowable, indeed desirable, that Catholics should join in prayer with their separated brethren. Such prayers in common are . . . a genuine expression of the ties which still bind Catholics to their separated brethren." [3]

Question 7: Will we need to be baptized again as Catholics?

The Catholic Church does not require baptism for those who have already been baptized in the trinitarian formula. [4]

---

[3] Vatican Council II, *Unitatis Redintegratio*, no. 8, in *Vatican Council II: The Conciliar and Post Conciliar Documents*, ed. Austin Flannery, O.P. New Port, N.Y.: Costello Publishing Co., 1992.

[4] Although Mormon baptism is done in the trinitarian formula, it is not accepted as *valid* baptism because of their theological view of the Trinity existing as "three Gods".

Those among us who had received water baptism "in Jesus' name" only would have to be baptized again.

Question 8: What if we were in a second marriage? Would we need to leave our present mates and return to our first spouses? And what about the children of that second marriage? Would they be declared illegitimate?

The Catholic Church does not require anyone to return to a previous marriage. Those involved in second marriages must submit their marital state to the Church's tribunal to determine which of their two marriages is valid. While Protestant marriages are valid in the eyes of the Church, there may be a "defect" as to their sacramentality. Such determinations are made after careful scrutiny by experts in canon law.

I was exhausted just thinking about all the possible questions I might need to deal with. I knew I had my work cut out for me, and I knew I needed more help.

The Process and the Problems

All these major changes that were occurring in my life, leading up to my entrance into the Catholic Church, took place over approximately a three-year period. I will be forever grateful for the people God connected me with during that time of formation.

The first, of course, was Professor Bill Riordan. Bill met with me, encouraged me in my studies, took me to my first Mass, and he and his wife, Claudia, had Donna and me over for dinner and answered countless questions. It was Bill who first introduced us to Steve Ray, a renowned Catholic apologist, Bible teacher, businessman, and author. Steve, his wife, Janet, and all four of their children were recent converts to the Catholic faith at that time. Since they live close by in the Ann Arbor area, it was easy to meet with Steve periodically for some in-depth discussions.

When Bill first called him and told him I was a Pentecostal pastor who was inquiring about the Catholic faith, Steve said, "I'll be right over!" He was on fire, and a trail of smoke followed him into the building. That started a great friendship. Steve invited us to come to his house on July 19, 1998, for a Sunday dinner with some of his friends.

Those friends included Father Ed Fride, pastor of Christ the King Church in Ann Arbor, himself a convert, and Al Kresta, Steve's best friend. Al had come back to the Catholic Church. His wife, Sally, and their first four children had converted to Catholicism. Their fifth child, David, is their first "cradle Catholic". Al is also a well-known Catholic apologist, author, and host of his own popular talk show, *Kresta in the Afternoon*, heard on Catholic radio stations across the country. I had met Al before, but it was prior to his "reversion," when he was an Evangelical and host of a talk show on WMUZ FM, a large Detroit Christian station.

Dennis Walters, the director of the RCIA (Rite of Christian Initiation of Adults) program at Christ the King, was also at that dinner. Dennis is an extraordinary man. As a catechist, he was willing to take the time to meet with Donna and me nearly every Tuesday for two full years.

Dennis started coming to our house on March 2, 1999, to begin our individualized RCIA classes. He would stop on his way home from work and stay for dinner. More than anyone else, he was key in my religious formation. We had some very deep discussions. I posed questions he had difficulty answering. I could challenge him, but he would come back with what the Church teaches. That was exactly what I needed because I had come to understand that the Magisterium had the authority to speak infallibly for Christ.

The pope wasn't difficult for me. That was one reason Catholicism was attractive to me. I had studied the early Church, and I understood that the early Church believed in the primacy of the bishop of Rome. The Church had the authority to do what she did. That made sense to me. The Bible could not be an authority in itself; it could only be an authority in the hands of someone competent enough to interpret it authoritatively. Just like the Constitution of the United States must have an authoritative body to interpret it, so the Bible alone cannot be an authority—it needs the infallible application of an interpretive body—the Church. Without an interpretive body, the Bible's meaning is anybody's guess. This is the reason there are more than thirty

thousand denominations that stand on their unique interpretation of the Bible as *the truth*. Thirty-three thousand
churches have proclaimed themselves to be *the church* that
can speak authoritatively about the Bible. Saint Paul wrote
to Timothy that the Church (not the Bible!) was "the pillar
and bulwark of the truth" (1 Tim 3:15).

In January 1999, I went to a Rite of Acceptance at Christ
the King Church. By mid-1999, I knew the Catholic Church
was *the* Church of Jesus Christ, the Church of the New Testament. This was the Church of the apostles, of the martyrs,
and of the saints. This was the Church of the faith that had
evolved and developed for more than two thousand years.

In order to receive the fullness of the Christian faith, I
knew I had to make that next step. That's when I accepted
Steve Ray's invitation to go to Steubenville, Ohio, for the
"Defending the Faith" conference at Franciscan University
in July. It absolutely blew me away. Here were Catholics
worshipping with an enthusiasm and love I had never before
witnessed in a Catholic gathering—and so many of them
too!

I came back from that and wrote to Cardinal Adam Maida
of the Archdiocese of Detroit about coming into the Catholic Church. To my disappointment, it was some three
months before anyone from the archdiocese contacted me.

Family Matters

While my enthusiasm for discovering the early Church grew
by leaps and bounds, my family and many of my friends
began to have serious doubts about my sanity.

Years before, I had purchased a little book on church
history at a book sale for just a dollar. It was probably the
best purchase I ever made. I had started reading it then, but

when it got too complicated, I put it away and didn't pick it up again until ten years later. After dusting it off, I read that the Greek Orthodox church had the earliest form of Christian worship, going back to the fourth century. I thought I would really like to see that.

I spoke with the pastor of Saints Constantine and Helen Greek Orthodox Church in Westland about my interest. The pastor there, Father Stephen, invited me to lunch. I told him I was fascinated with early Christian worship. He was ecstatic and told me he was giving a workshop for four Wednesday evenings explaining the Greek liturgy to his own parishioners, since many of the young people didn't really understand it. He invited me to come. So in November of 1998, I brought one of my technical people with me, and we taped all four sessions.

I felt as though I had gone back into apostolic times. He went into detail explaining how the ceremony begins a half hour before the people come; how they pray before they vest; how they bless their garments and put the chasuble on; and how they prepare the Eucharist behind the screen from a large loaf of bread with the center cut out. It was all very fascinating to me. So in March 1999, I convinced Donna to attend a service with me.

She thought I was crazy. But I left my church in the hands of one of my deacons one Sunday and took Donna to Saints Constantine and Helen Greek Orthodox Church. To make matters worse, Donna is allergic to incense, and the Orthodox use incense heavily. They sat Donna in the front row and invited me to come behind the screen. I was fascinated. During the consecration, the priest's back is to the congregation to symbolize the mystery of God in heaven. The priest periodically hits the ground, symbolizing humility before God.

I peeked out from behind the screen to see what the priest sees when he looks out on his parishioners, and some of the people, catching sight of me, had surprised looks on their faces. I looked at Donna, and she appeared confused and was crossing herself with her left hand.

When the worshippers come to receive the Eucharist, they take a piece of the bread back to their seat with them and, as they go back, they kiss the icon of the Blessed Mother. That was quite unnerving to my wife.

Donna and I stayed for fellowship after the service, and I was offered an opportunity to be a priest in the Orthodox church. I told them I would think about it. I had loved the liturgy and the solemnity of the service, but by then I had discovered the seat of Peter.

When we got home, Donna called my sister and told her I was losing my mind. She thought I was having a nervous breakdown. I found out later that Donna went over to my sister's house that day, and they prayed for me because they thought I was becoming very unstable. Donna was also worried because she found nothing wrong with the faith she had. She had no interest in learning about another faith because God was real to her in her own faith. Why would she want to even think about another one?

As I dug deeper into the early Fathers of the Church, Donna became even more antagonistic. I just continued to read and make changes in our worship service. I created my own sacramentary and my own reading schedule. Slowly I began to change our readings into the readings of the Church. I began to use the eucharistic prayers and the prefaces, and my wife was just sinking more and more into despair.

In June, we went on a cruise to Jamaica. Most think of a cruise as a time for romance, but it was a time for intense study for me. There is no time for romance when you are uncovering the well of living waters. I knew Donna was upset. My sister was upset. Everybody was upset. But I couldn't stop what I had started.

Donna and I argued often, sometimes until three o'clock in the morning. There was a rift between us. It was difficult for her, and she was determined to prove the error of my ways. That was probably what enticed her to read some of the materials I was reading—she was searching for the ammunition to shoot holes in Catholic teaching.

She was downright hostile at the dinner at Steve Ray's house that July of 1998 and got into a heated discussion with Al Kresta about Mary and Purgatory and Catholics not living their faith. But her mind was closed, and they couldn't budge her. Later she told me, "I'll never accept that—that's junk!"

By the summer of 1999, after attending the conference at Steubenville, I was convinced that I would become Catholic. I could see that Donna was impressed and moved as well.

As much as I would like to say that I was the one who convinced Donna to come into the Church, I can't. My arguments were meaningless to her. I could never convince her. It was her own study in an effort to disprove the authenticity of Catholicism and the Holy Spirit putting it into her heart that she should come into the Church. I was in my den one day, working on the computer while watching a video of an Orthodox liturgy. I called to Donna to come and watch the video with me. She was agitated and expressed her disapproval, but eventually came in and sat down. She was quiet for a few minutes, then turned to me and said, "Al, I'm Catholic. Send an e-mail to Steve Ray, and tell him I'm Catholic."

She knew she would lose a lot too—her friends, her office in the church, her work, and her ministry would all be gone. Her decision was monumental. But she told me she had had a conversation with God. She said the Lord had asked her: Will you come into my Church? She said: Yes!

The Boys

When Donna and I had both determined to become Catholic, we had a big roundtable meeting after dinner one Sunday evening with our three boys and their wives. They were members of my church and had been involved in all the changes I was making. They liked the apostolic tradition and the changes toward apostolic worship. Our oldest son, Joseph, was even studying for the ministry. But when we told them we had decided to become Catholic, they thought we were nuts. It went over like a brick.

My two oldest sons had the most problems with my intentions. They didn't want us to become Catholic for a variety of reasons. Joseph was getting ready for ministry. He realized that if he became Catholic he could never be ordained. He would never be a preacher. All that would be lost to him if he came into the Church. That was a very big sacrifice he would have to make if he chose to enter the Catholic Church.

Ben didn't want me to become Catholic because, he reasoned, "You're not going to have a chance to preach in the Catholic Church. You're going to get pushed aside and you're going to lose your ministry. Why would you give up all you have worked so hard for?" It just didn't make sense to him. Plus, to come into a White man's church was nearly unthinkable for him. He realized that we would be giving up all our cultural amenities—our music, our approach, our theology. Why would we do that? He couldn't see going into a White institution that had proven itself to be anti-Black and insensitive (much of this was based on problems he had had with White police officers during his youth). And here I was saying to him: "Yes, but this is the Church of Jesus Christ!"

He finally said to me, "I have faith in you, Dad. And if you say this is Christ's Church, I'll accept it, not because I see it, but because I believe you." My youngest son, Marc, didn't have much to say, but he listened.

I told them that I realized the Catholic Church has evil people in it. It has racists in it. It has people in it that bring great shame to it. That, I told them, was irrelevant. I was a pastor, and I knew that every congregation, every church has good and bad. Every church is part of society. I have heard everything and every kind of confession.

Still, I think it was sad for them because they knew I would have to give up my ministry. Joseph hoped that if Cardinal Maida would allow me to enter the priesthood, he would be able to enter the priesthood. I kept telling him, "You're not going to be able to become a priest. You must accept that fact." I told him there are other things that you can be within the Church, other ways to be of service—as a catechist, a lector, a eucharistic minister, or a deacon. But he wanted so badly to be a shepherd. It was very difficult for him to give up on that dream. I am so grateful that they trusted me and began to ask questions and allowed me to explain the truths about the Church I had uncovered.

Maranatha

I called the church together the first Sunday of January 2000 after the Sunday worship, and I told the people there what

I had been doing and what I had discovered. I told them, "If you will allow me six months, I will share with you what I have learned. I will tell you how we have been lied to about the Catholic Church. I will explain what I have learned about the Church, and I will try to answer all your questions."

There were about 150 people there that Sunday, and when I said, "If you will allow me six months' time to teach and answer questions about the Catholic faith, stand up", everyone stood up. And I thought to myself, "Thank you, Jesus! I get a salary next week." But, of course, it was so much more than that.

Some of them never came back, but many did stay and give me that opportunity to teach. Many felt I was using poor judgment, but they really loved me and were determined to stay until, and if, the time came for me to enter the Church.

And so began a six-month series of classes I taught about the Catholic Church.

I had been teaching about the history of the Church at our Wednesday night studies for about a year and a half with no thought of being Catholic. After I made the announcement, Wednesday nights became a time to teach the truths of the Catholic faith and answer, to the best of my ability, those questions that were troubling my people. On Sunday I would just preach the Word of God.

Two Great Friends

During this period of transition, two previously ordained ministers, Michael Orr and Michael Williams, joined the Maranatha family. They proved to be invaluable as supporters and close friends. Michael Orr and his wife Tanya came to us about halfway through our transition. He was a valuable asset to us because of his knowledge of Eastern Orthodoxy and his skill as a musician. Michael's affinity with the Orthodox church gave him a good feel for liturgy. With his skill in music, he was able to take the structure of Latin Liturgy and "African-Americanize" it so that our Sunday morning worship was not only liturgically "by the book", but culturally acceptable to our congregation. Unfortunately, neither Michael nor Tanya entered the Church with us, but I will always be grateful for their support and good will.

Michael Williams was a Pentecostal minister, but had been raised a Catholic by his mother. His knowledge of the Catholic faith helped me to better understand the "cultural" aspect of Catholicism. His spiritual insights and prophetic words about our transition to Catholicism have come true beyond our wildest imagination. He and his musically talented wife, Amiesha, also declined to come with us into the Catholic Church, but as with Michael Orr, I will always carry in my heart a deep love and appreciation for their unwavering support.

II

The Struggle

Do not think that I have come to bring peace to the earth; I have not come to bring peace, but a sword. For I have come to set a man against his father, and a daughter against her mother, and a daughter-in-law against her mother-in-law; and a man's foes will be those of his own household. He who loves father or mother more than me is not worthy of me; and he who loves son or daughter more than me is not worthy of me; and he who does not take up his cross and follow me is not worthy of me. He who finds his life will lose it, and he who loses his life for my sake will find it (Mt 10:34–39).

While Dennis Walters continued catechizing Donna and me in preparation to enter the Church and I continued teaching my congregation, I remained disappointed that the Detroit Archdiocese had not contacted me immediately after receiving my letter of intent to enter the Church. Now I better understand the archdiocese's caution in wanting me and anyone that would follow me into the Church to be certain of his actions. There would also be issues that would need to be resolved regarding divorce and other situations.

But, at the time, the archdiocesan silence was a great disappointment. I understood quickly that this was not going to be easy. As an Evangelical, if a Catholic priest had come to me interested in joining *my* church, I would have beaten a path to his door. I would have brought him to the church, introduced him to the people, and gotten him involved in the prayer life and the social life of the church. I would have worked with him step-by-step and taught him how to disentangle himself from his church and become part of ours.

None of that took place for me. It seemed to me to be as cold as an iceberg. There was no enthusiasm. I was feeling such tremendous joy in my discovery of this Church, and I soon realized I had to rejoice in just what I was learning because I didn't know anyone else that was doing this except for Steve Anderson, a friend I had met a few years back at a pastors' conference.

Steve was the pastor of the Charismatic Episcopal Church in Brighton, Michigan (the CEC is not affiliated with the historical Episcopal Church). He had recently graduated from Oral Roberts University and had intended to start a nondenominational church, but, like me, he too stumbled across the Church Fathers and found it necessary to rethink his plans. He sought to identify with apostolic Christianity by combining the practices of liturgical church with his charismatic past. He eventually resigned from his pastorate and entered Sacred Heart Major Seminary in Detroit in 2000. Although married, with papal permission, he went on to become an ordained priest in the Diocese of Lansing.

It was through Steve that I found out there were more out there like us. It was wonderful to find out that I wasn't just a nut. It was happening everywhere to all kinds of pastors. Many, however, stopped at the Orthodox church, but I had already discovered the seat of Peter. For me, there was no stopping. And while I still have a love for the beauty of the Byzantine Rite, the Saint John Chrysostom Rite, and the Saint James Rite, I could never bring those to my people. In addition to understanding the primacy of Peter, the cultural differences were just too great.

I knew there would still be significant cultural differences to adjust to. Pentecostal worship, even though ours had become a more dignified, civilized form of worship, was filled with joyful music, hand-clapping, and swaying back and forth. It was a Spirit-filled worship felt with body, mind, and soul.

When I was in Africa at a very large Catholic conference in 2003, I saw much the same kind of worship. It was dynamic, and it was loud and joyous and filled with praise. But when it came time for the Consecration, everything changed. The reverent way the priest handled the Eucharist, how he said the words, how he elevated the host so everyone could see, brought an awe-filled hush to the thousands present. Instead of ringing bells during the elevation, the African tradition is that everyone claps.

But it is so different in the United States. Catholicism came to this country through nationalities—the Italians, the Irish, the Polish—and they were White, and they brought their culture and their Catholicism to this country, and that is what defines Catholic worship in this country. Unfortunately African Americans were totally outside the walls when this was happening. Today, however, there are more Blacks in the Catholic Church than in the Baptist or Methodist churches. In fact, worldwide, there are two hundred million Black Catholics—making Catholicism the largest religion in the world for people of African descent.

Still, some of the reactions I got when Catholics found out I was coming into the Church were disheartening. One priest actually asked why I would *want* to come into the Church. And there were other Catholics who expressed similar sentiments. There was no universal concept. They felt everyone has his own religion, and it works for him—so great! They believed the unity lies in the belief in God and in Jesus Christ, not in the governmental unity of the Church. Hey, we're all going to heaven, so just stay where you are!

They are trying to be magnanimous. What they failed to
realize is that when a person's heart has been stirred to see
the truth of the Church, that kind of thinking comes across
almost as that of an apostate. They had no idea what they
were telling me to do! I was willing to disrupt my entire
life to become Catholic, and here they were telling me that
I didn't need to do that. It showed me at what level they
were. They revealed that they were in the Church, but the
Church was not really in their hearts. That's religious
indifferentism.

I don't think those people know what they are saying. It
is a tremendous hindrance to tell someone seeking the truth
to stay where he is. By doing so, they are depriving the
seeker of the Lord's Table. Some think that sharing the truths
of the Catholic Church is proselytizing. I would say to them
that it would be proselytizing if they went to someone's
house, popped in his door, and said, "You have to become
Catholic to be saved", or simply "You need to become
Catholic."

If someone asks me what it means to be Catholic and I
tell him—that is not proselytizing. If a person has no religious tradition at all and I tell him—Christ loves you, come
on down to Saints Peter and Paul Church, and we'll help
you find a relationship with Christ and we'll baptize you—
that is not proselytizing. That is evangelizing, something
Pope John Paul II called upon us all to do. But many people confuse that with proselytizing, and they have the mis-
taken idea that feeding the poor people peanut butter and
jelly sandwiches and hot coffee is evangelization. That is
not evangelization. That is the work of the Church—the
mission of the Church is to serve the poor. Evangelization
means renewal of the inner man with the Word of Christ,
the teachings of Christ. The core of evangelization is bringing

about conversion—an inner conversion brought about by the Holy Spirit through a grace-filled moment to a life more conforming to the image of Christ.

And that conversion is a process—as I discovered—that is sometimes filled with doubt, especially as friends and family turn their backs on you and leave. All of my ministers left. I think the most difficult part was to see those very close to me walk away. One of my deacons, Clarence Ewing, a good and holy man, was closer than a brother to me. We had knocked on doors together; we had lain before the presence of God together; we had suffered together. But as I taught about Catholicism, he remained absent from church for about three months. One Tuesday morning, during our eleven o'clock prayer service, he walked in. I thought maybe he was coming back. I said, "I'm so glad to see you, Deacon!" But when he asked to see me for a moment, I knew.

He walked into my office and said, "I love you, Pastor, but I cannot follow you." Then he wrote me a check for his missed offerings and walked away. I never saw him in church again. That was extremely painful. But the most painful to me personally were the reactions from my family.

During this time of learning, teaching, discerning, and dealing with loved ones' reactions, I would often wake up at two or three o'clock in the morning, and I would literally wrestle in my mind with, "Why am I doing this? I must be really off my rocker now. Am I losing my mind?"

It was absolutely horrible. I would wake up in a total panic. I had battles with my own self—with my own thoughts. I had battles with family and friends. And then, what would come to my mind was that initial discovery: This is the Church. And I would tell myself, "Okay, that's why I am doing this." That's the only thing that really kept me together. And then each night there would be a repeat.

There was very little sleep as I continued to wrestle with the question: Am I doing the right thing?

Often after services on Sundays, we—including family from other churches—would gather at one family member's house for dinner. We didn't talk about sports or politics. We would talk about what God was doing and about his Word, and then we would have good prayer and go home.

On this one particular Sunday I was really, really depressed. I was at my lowest point ever as I continued to wrestle with my own judgment. Here I was destroying my own ministry and wondering why it was that I could so clearly see the truth of the Catholic Church. As far as I knew then, there were no other pastors in the city that saw what I saw. There were pastors far more educated, far holier than I was. Why didn't they see this? Why was I doing this and they weren't? Was I actually making a bad judgment choice?

I was voicing my concerns out loud to Donna as we were on our way to my sister's house for dinner. That day my cousin, Dave Winans, and his wife also came by. They are the Mom and Pop Winans in the famous gospel singing group.

When we arrived at Gwen's house, I could see that she had been crying. She told me, "Brother, I love you, but I'm not going into the Catholic Church. No way!" She was the treasurer at my church and a great administrator.

I was devastated, but I simply said, "Okay, just give the books to your assistant."

Then my niece, who was also my worship leader, walked in. "There is no way that I'm going to become Catholic either", Linda told me.

I said, "Okay. You do what you have to."

Then my own mother came strutting in and said, "And I ain't becoming Catholic. God told me to be holy; he didn't tell me to be Catholic!"

Thankfully Donna and our boys and their families were with me at this point, but it was painfully apparent that the rest of my family was not.

These exchanges had already taken place by the time Dave and his wife arrived. He had heard that things were going on at my church and that people were leaving, but he didn't know why. He knew I was a good pastor.

I couldn't say the prayer that day, so I asked Dave to pray. After he prayed, he came over and laid hands on me and gave a prophetic blessing. He said, "Keep doing what you are doing. Keep teaching what you teach. Teach holy living. If you stop, what will your enemies say?"

Then, in the name of the Lord, he uttered the most prophetic words, "For I am with you."

It was like the weight of the world was lifted from my shoulders when I heard that God was with me. I felt that I wasn't nuts. I knew that what I was doing was purposeful. It was a bigger design than what I had drawn.

After the prayer, my sister came to me and said, "Well, if the Lord is with you, then I'm not going anywhere." And my niece added, "I'm staying with you too."

When my cousin, Dave, realized what I was doing, he tried to repudiate that prophetic word. I asked him, "Are you saying the Holy Spirit wasn't using you?" To this day he is very hurt that I became Catholic because he is very anti-Catholic. You have to remember that we were taught the same anti-Catholic things by our pastor, who was his grandfather. Dave Winans is a dear, dear brother and loves the Lord and is a holy man, but he just can't accept this Catholic thing. He is so grieved that he is now somehow tied up with that and that I feel he encouraged me to come into the Catholic Church. It is a matter of salvation to him, and he feels that we have made a tragic mistake.

He has said to me, "Catholics might be saved because they don't know any better. But you—you know better, and you have turned your back on your faith and on holiness and now you have gone into something that is just not true."

So I am an apostate. In his eyes, I am an apostate. In many people's eyes, I am an apostate. In their eyes, I have walked away from the truth. In reality, I walked into the truth. So I balanced the deep pains of rejection from my friends and relatives with the joy of discovery in finding that truth. That's the only thing that sustained me.

Perhaps the greatest pain in my becoming Catholic was the inability of my saintly mother to comprehend what I had done. Even in her declining years she fervently fasted and prayed that I might return to the Pentecostal church. As she advanced into her nineties and as her memory began to fade, she would repeatedly ask me, "Son, what church do you belong to?" It was so painful to see the sorrow etched on her face when I answered her, "Catholic, Ma, I'm in the Catholic Church." She could not understand why I would leave the faith of my fathers to "go to something not of God". She died at the age of 94, never reconciled to the fact that what I had done was the will of God.

12

The Vote

A response from the Detroit Archdiocese finally arrived about three months after I had written to Cardinal Maida about my intentions to become Catholic. I received a letter on October 26, 1999, offering an appointment to meet with Father John Buddy, the archdiocesan ecumenical officer. I was made aware that the archdiocese would approach our situation with great caution. I met with Father Buddy several times by the end of that year, and I could see things were going to progress very slowly.

As I continued teaching about the Catholic faith during the first few months of 2000, I watched my congregation dwindle from around two hundred members to about eighty. Some of them went away angry. Some of them probably felt betrayed. They had put their whole trust in me, and they just could not make that leap of faith. They could not see themselves going into a Church that they felt had nothing to offer them. No matter how I tried to explain things to them, they just could not see that, and some of them just didn't want to hear it. They told me, "I was born this way and I will die this way." And they left.

Bishop Moses Anderson, Detroit's only African-American bishop and one of only fourteen in the United States, attended a Sunday service at Maranatha during that time of learning and discernment. After the service, he answered questions. He told those gathered that the bishops of Detroit were excited about what was going on at Maranatha. To me, however, it seemed like the archdiocese was still dragging its feet.

I believe, at the time, the archdiocese really didn't know what to do with me and my congregation. The Catholic Church in Detroit is very ecumenical, and the cardinal has many friends of all faiths. The pastors are like a consortium, and they work well together. I think there was some concern about how this congregation's becoming Catholic would look to other Christians. I believe there may have been a fear that the Church would be considered triumphalistic and that might upset the balance in the city. The archdiocese really wasn't sure how to handle the situation. Bishop Anderson, himself a convert to the faith, asked to be the one to work with me since he had a pretty good idea of what I was going through.

So I met with Bishop Anderson two or three times, and he answered my questions very diplomatically, every word weighed so as not to give the wrong impression and not to betray the office of bishop or the Church in Detroit. The archdiocese was careful to keep a low profile, while I was just bursting at the seams.

During that time I wrote a letter to Cardinal Adam Maida. "Why aren't you saying anything?" I asked. "Your Eminence, your silence is greater than the persecution we are getting from our friends." I was very frustrated, but I persevered. I had no choice. This was the Church of the New Testament.

After three months of Catholic catechesis, I felt in my heart it needed to stop. During our Tuesday morning prayer service one day, a Scripture passage came to mind. In 1 Samuel 10:27, when Saul was chosen to be the first king of Israel, people brought him gifts, but there were those who did not, and Saul simply "held his peace". In other words, the decision had been made. I felt I was in the same position as Saul, and so I stopped.

From that point on I just preached. Wednesday nights became a time to teach spiritual principles. I felt those who would come into the Church with me had already made up their minds to do so. Those who had decided against it would not be changed by anything more I could say.

And so it was that on June 4, 2000, the feast of the Ascension of the Lord—a Sunday celebrating Christian unity— the congregants filed through the big wooden doors of Maranatha and dropped their yellow ballots into the box. The question: Do you want to take the next steps necessary to enter the Catholic Church?

Only fifty-eight voted that day and, of those, thirty-nine voted yes. When the results were announced, applause erupted from the congregation. But, for me, the victory was bittersweet. There were the nineteen that had voted no. And seeing people I loved walk away because they didn't understand was one of the most painful aspects of the entire process. Sixty-two members seriously considered becoming Catholic and, in the end, a total of fifty-four members of the Maranatha congregation decided to become Catholic. I was amazed and pleased there were that many.

We learned from the archdiocese that we would be assumed into Saint Suzanne's in Detroit where we would also be enrolled in the RCIA program. Father Dennis Duggan, Saint Suzanne's pastor, was very excited. He came by to see us several times during our Sunday morning liturgy and to speak with us. In his excitement, he made one major mistake. He told the people of Saint Suzanne that they were going to merge with a Pentecostal church. What they heard was: We're going to become Pentecostal. Father Dennis was never totally able to straighten that out.

We sold the Maranatha property on July 7, 2000, to the Church of God in Christ and, after paying off the mortgage and other expenses, there was more than $500,000 profit. According to Michigan's nonprofit laws, we had to give the money to charities and 501(c)(3) organizations. So we drew up a list of nonprofit organizations we felt were really helping people to better their lives and mailed them $20,000 checks. I received a severance package that would sustain me until I could find another job. After selling the church, we were allowed to meet at Bishop Borgess High School as a group through the summer. During that time, we were visited by members of Saint Suzanne's. Some were very welcoming and came to say they were so glad to have us join their church. "You'll revive us", they said. But others came to warn us: "You're not going to change anything. Don't think you're going to change anything."

We were excited about coming in, but that was a little disconcerting. We wondered why they warned us not to try changing them. We were not even hoping to change them. We just wanted to be Catholic.

And that was our sole intent as we marched into Saint Suzanne's on September 10, 2000, singing "Blessed Assurance". I presented my robes to Father Dennis, and said, "These are the robes I give to the Church. If they are given back to me to serve, I will serve. Whatever the Church wants me to do, I will do." There was still a part of me hoping against hope that I might serve the Church as a priest even though I knew the chances were slim.

While many of the parishioners were very accepting of us as we began attending Sunday services at Saint Suzanne's, there were those that definitely did not want us there. Some left to go to another church. Some started going to Mass on Saturday so as not to worship with us on Sunday. I more or less expected some racism. I knew this was a perfect Church with imperfect people. I knew that part of the imperfection would be based in fear or ambivalence or racism. After all, an institution this old and this large has to have some fleas! Yet the Church is perfect. She is sanctified and holy. As Saint Augustine pointed out, the Church is holy because of her purposes, not because of her people. We are sinners in the throes of transformation, being transformed to be as Christ is. I understood that because of the presence of the Holy Spirit, the Church is holy, but not necessarily the people.

There were sixty-two of us that started in the RCIA program that fall (in the end, fifty-four of us actually became Catholic). Saint Suzanne's—in fact no other Catholic church in the city, state, or country—had experienced anything quite like this. And the people there weren't ready for us. They didn't know how to handle us. We knew the faith. We knew and loved God. We had experienced God. I had taught the Catholic faith to them straight from the *Catechism of the Catholic Church*; straight from the Church Fathers; straight from Vatican II.

They didn't have a clue about what we needed! We were so far advanced in our Christian experience, and they didn't know how to deal with us. The first lesson they taught was: "Who is God?" We already had knowledge of God and a tremendous knowledge of the Word of God. We were not catechumens, we were candidates. What they failed to understand was that our lives had been altered by an encounter with the resurrected Christ. Some of the people had been delivered from drugs. Some had been supernaturally healed, and they had developed a deep relationship with Christ. We had gotten the God thing down. We knew he existed because he had been operating in our lives, and we

ALEX' STORY

recognized his presence. We loved him so much we could hardly stand it! What we didn't know was all that the Church teaches. We realized we had missed out on a lot, so we kept asking them to teach us what the Church teaches. But that's not what we got.

One time an ex-priest came in to teach our class. By this time, we had come to see the Eucharist truly as the Body of our Lord and the Blood of our Lord, and it was very, very special and very, very sacred to us. This ex-priest began making wisecracks about how the Host was dry as a bone and would stick to the roof of your mouth. We were very offended. We never wanted him to come back because, to us, he had desecrated the very idea of the Eucharist. We had come through so much, and our intensity and level of commitment was so much deeper than what they were teaching us. It was about that time that I realized we were coming into a Church in which many didn't embrace all of the Church's teachings. That was hard because we had expected these people to exhibit so much spirituality. After all, they had the sacraments, the Eucharist, the fullness of the faith, and we felt it would be more evident in their lives. That was disappointing.

We had come from a faith that was so serious to us—it was life and death. It controlled our lives. Everything we did, we did in the name of the Lord Jesus Christ. What we experienced seemed to be a people who cared less about God and his Church than we did. Whatever we did, we did out of love for Christ. Faith was the center of our lives— not a part of our lives—but the center of our lives.

Still, going through RCIA built anticipation for receiving the Eucharist. The joy of just being in the Church over-shadowed all the negatives. We knew we were coming into full union with the Church of Jesus Christ.

During that time, I asked Cardinal Maida again about the possibility of becoming a priest in the Catholic Church, and he very diplomatically and very "Catholically" said, "No." Still, I harbored some hope. But when Bishop Moses Anderson pointed out that typically married men serve the Church in the permanent diaconate, I knew then not to push it. I decided I didn't have a snowball's chance in hell of becoming a priest. And I really didn't think about becoming a deacon at that time. I just set my sights on learning the faith—all I had missed for so many years—all there was to learn. The fullness of the faith: just listen to those words—*the fullness of the faith!* You can only appreciate it when you realize you've had only partial faith for so long. What we had was good, but now this was the whole enchilada!

There were definitely some barriers in coming into a European Anglo-Saxon Church. There is an African and an Eastern version of the Church, but we live in the Americas where it is a European Catholic Church. Those were barriers we had to cross. That knowledge of becoming one with the Church of Jesus Christ was what sustained us through some of the more difficult aspects of our first year at Saint Suzanne's. Father Dennis worked very hard to make us feel welcome. He brought in African-American hymnals with African-American songs along with traditional Catholic songs. The choir grew from five to twenty-five as some of our people joined. They would sing one or two of the African-American songs during the service, but they would sing them as though they were, well, dying! When African Americans sing, it is an act of worship, an expression of our faith. After about a month, the choir dwindled back down to five. Still, we continued with our quest to become part of this Church.

We persevered to the following April. We had been criticized and ostracized. We had spent three years in preparation; studying, answering questions, and watching our friends
melt away. But on April 14, 2001, the night of the Easter
Vigil, that feeling of fighting through miles and miles and
miles of jungle was about to come to an end. It was like
discovering the South Pole—going through those dreary
nights and days of pulling the load, not knowing if you
were going to make it; holding out hope—and finally we
were there!

It was the end of the beginning and the beginning of
our new life in the Catholic Church.

13

Home at Last

The night of the Easter Vigil, April 14, 2001, I felt the greatest sense of relief. I had finally traversed those difficult roads of discovery, of rejection, of uncertainty, of not knowing who would come into the Church with me, of not knowing if we could really pull this off.

But here we were—fifty-two of us entering the Catholic Church, holding our candles and getting ready to march in. My wife, our three sons and their wives and children, my sister, my niece, and other family members were all standing there with me. Two more members of the Maranatha family entered the Church the following day on Easter Sunday. Three of our members had already come back to the Church, having only to go to confession before receiving the Eucharist again. We also had a few newborn babies during the year that had been baptized in the Church and so were members before we were.

But that night of the Easter Vigil was the most holy night for the rest of us. We met downstairs before the service began. Steve and Janet Ray were there. Janet was Donna's sponsor, and Dennis Walters was mine. Father Clarence Williams, C.P.P.S., director of the Office for Black Catholic Ministries for the Archdiocese of Detroit, was there. We had a bit of a preliminary pep rally before going upstairs. I told them that this was it. "We've done it!" I said. "We've pulled it off!" All that we had been preparing for over the last two years was about to come to fruition.

We went upstairs and, as we processed into the church, I was thinking, "This is the most beautiful night of my life." I would finally become what I had sought for so long. I had imitated Catholics. I had imitated Catholic liturgy. And now it was time to become truly Catholic, to become one with the Church, to come home. And that is exactly how I felt—that I was finally coming home.

The Paschal candle, representing the Light of Christ, was lit before we entered the darkened church. Father Dennis three times said, "Christ our light." Our response was, "Thanks be to God." On the second response our candles were lit and we processed into the church behind the Pascal candle. It was absolutely beautiful as our candles lighted our procession into the church, filled with some five hundred to six hundred people. Saint Suzanne's hadn't been that full in years! The singing was beautiful. Looking back on this now, I realize that all along I had been following the light of Christ. As we entered the darkened church, it symbolically portrayed our journey of faith from glory to glory, from the knowledge of redemption to a greater and more profound mystery of the resurrected Christ.

Then it came time for the baptisms of some of our people who had not received proper baptisms in the trinitarian formula. They had been baptized only in the name of the Lord Jesus, which is not a valid baptism.

Next came our oath of allegiance to the Church. We were required to come as individuals and families to say it. I was, of course, the first one. I recall standing by the altar with all of my family and friends and feeling such a sense of pride as I said, "I believe all that the Catholic Church teaches, preaches, and proclaims."

Then we lined up in a huge semi-circle around the altar, and it stretched from one side of the church to the other. It was awesome as Father Dennis Duggan confirmed us and anointed each of us with the oil of chrism and said, "Receive the Holy Spirit." For me, it was nothing short of miraculous. I was crying when he anointed me, and I said to him, "Father Dennis, I'm finally home!" That was precisely how I felt. I was home, and now I could start anew. All my journeys, decisions, and searchings for the truth were finally behind me. It was such a feeling of relief. It was a feeling that only a son who has been away from home for a long time and who has finally come back to the family can feel. I felt like a sojourner, like a wanderer who had finally, by Providence, found a way home. This was exactly where I was supposed to be—where God had been leading me all through my life. This was the night it was completed. As it is said in the Passover: This was the night of all nights. I had it all. I had been baptized in the faith as a child, brought up in the faith of the Lord, and here I was, now united in the fullness of the faith.

I felt such excitement to come into the Church of Jesus Christ. To this very day, I am still excited. This is the Church of Peter and Paul, the Church of the apostles, the Church of history. All of it belonged to me from that moment on. All the saints, all the martyrs, all the holy men and women of the Church were now part of me. I was now in complete union. I could come no closer to it than this. I was incredibly happy.

Before the ceremony began, I had asked Father Dennis if I could receive Communion on my knees just for this first time. He graciously allowed me to do so. And as I knelt before our Lord and received him into myself for the first time, I was incredibly moved.

This was my God, who humbled himself for me that I might have life more abundantly. And I understood—not because I went to a seminary and studied sacramental theology—but because I had read the Church Fathers, what the Church has always testified, that the Eucharist is the source and summit of the faith. I understood that. Those years, those weeks and months when I was not allowed to take our Lord's Body and Blood, I developed an intense longing for him. I had him spiritually for more than forty years, but to have him in the Eucharist—to touch him and eat him sacramentally, physically, substantially—that was powerful. I was willing to walk away from my previous life—from family, friends, ministry, leadership, livelihood, everything—for that alone.

If there was to be any regret, it was that I had not learned the truth earlier. Why couldn't I have known all this in my youth or early adulthood?

And so every weekday morning, immediately after I came into the Church, I would go to Blessed Sacrament Monastery on Middlebelt Road in Farmington Hills, and I would participate in seven o'clock Mass with the cloistered nuns and say the Liturgy of the Hours with them. Then I would stay afterward to pray and to ask God questions that had me puzzled.

I wanted to know why he would call me to his Church so late in life. Why? Why did this happen to me now? Why didn't I see the truth of the Catholic Church when I was in my twenties or thirties? I could have given my entire life to it. And why was I able to see this truth when other Protestant ministers, far more intelligent, far more gifted, far more educated, and far more holy than I am, didn't see it? How had I stumbled upon this—a man who is very ordinary in every sense of the word? It was so plain to me—as though it had just peeled back and was revealed to me. I saw the truth so clearly. Why couldn't these intelligent, gifted Protestant pastors see this?

It wasn't until I began to travel and meet people face to face that I began to understand why. It was as if the Lord had said, "I can show you better than I can tell you."

As I began to travel around the country speaking at churches and conferences, I saw the great thirst and hunger for knowledge of the faith among Catholics. They wanted to know their faith. They really wanted a relationship with Jesus Christ. Without that, their faith seemed superficial to them.

I began to see the breadth and the dimension of those who are converts and those coming into the Church. I began to meet those—hundreds of them—who had come into the Church pretty much the same way I did. I began to realize that my conversion was not unique. It was a typical conversion, maybe a bit more public, but it was a typical conversion.

People become Catholic because they have discovered the authenticity of the Catholic faith, generally through three different avenues: they recognize the authority of the Church; they have discovered the Blessed Mother; or they have studied the Church Fathers. The more I traveled, the more people I met, the more I began to realize that God is at work renewing his Church. He is stirring the cradle Catholics, and he is bringing in converts who have a relationship with him, a profound love of God, to build up the faith of the Church, to strengthen it.

As I began to realize this, I felt a sense of profound humility that he would think of me and add me to that number. He could have chosen anyone else, but he chose—or called—me. Maybe he called others, and they said No—I don't know. All I know is that I said Yes.

I had been satisfied with being Protestant. I loved my faith. I loved my church. I loved my position and my life the way it was. But when the truth of the Catholic Church was revealed to me, I had no real choice. I could not continue as a purveyor of truth if I found truth and then walked away from it! I had to embrace it no matter how difficult it was. And it was difficult.

Now I see that God is doing a wonderful work in his Church, and I am just a very, very small part of it. God is touching men and women, Black and White, all races from all walks of life, and bringing them into his Church. He is renewing the life of his Church and the joys of his salvation.

The negative things going on in the Church are far outweighed by the good that is being done. As Saint Paul says: Where sin abounds, grace abounds that much more.[1] That's what keeps the Church afloat. The spirit of holiness is in the Church. It is the spirit of Christ. It is the Holy Spirit, the soul of the Church that manifests itself in those who say Yes to him. I said Yes. I love being a Catholic Christian. I love the Church and her priests and her sacraments. I love the liturgy, the depth of spirituality, and the Church's commitment to life, human dignity, and peace and justice. All I ask of the Church is the opportunity to live out my days in study, prayer, and ministry to the poor. I have no agenda, no cause, and no point to prove. I do not seek position or favor, just the opportunity to serve without fanfare or recognition.

I'm home at last!

---

[1] "Then as one man's [Adam's] trespass led to condemnation for all men, so one man's [Jesus'] act of righteousness leads to aquittal and life for all men. For as by one man's disobedience many were made sinners, so by one man's obedience many will be made righteous. Law came in, to increase the trespass; *but where sin increased, grace abounded all the more*, so that, as sin reigned in death, grace also might reign through righteousness to eternal life through Jesus Christ our Lord (Rom 5:18–21, italics added).

14

Now What?

When I came into the Catholic Church, I had no plans. I didn't know what to think about my future. I just walked in the door and thought: I'm here. Now what?

I remember telling Dennis Walters that I had no desire to be a public figure, to be famous. I just wanted to learn more about this tremendous faith I had discovered. My initial thoughts were that perhaps I would go back to teaching and spend the rest of my life learning about my faith and maybe working with the poor. That was it. I was just going to prepare to meet my Maker by helping others and atoning for my sins. Never in my wildest dreams did I think I would be doing what I'm doing now.

My original thought, of course, was that I might become a priest—go to the seminary for five years and be assigned a parish—then all of us who had come from Maranatha could be together. That was *the* dream. But that was not to be. So my ministry, as I had known it, died when I became Catholic.

At first I was disappointed. Then I said to myself, whatever the Church asks me to do, I will do it. Now the ministry is the Lord's. I don't know where it's going to go or what I'm going to do. All I can say is that I just go where God opens the doors.

Shortly before I entered the Church, I gave a testimonial about my experiences on becoming Catholic at the Saint John's Center in Plymouth, Michigan. That was taped for

Saint Joseph Communications along with a dinner and casual conversation that followed. People bought the video, and it aired and still occasionally runs on EWTN, and the word spread about what was happening in Detroit. I started getting calls from parishes and organizations that wanted me to come and give my testimonial or talk about topics such as my conversion, the Church Fathers, life in the Spirit, the sacraments, and Mary the Mother of God. I have now developed about thirty topics that I have spoken about.

In the summer of 2002, Father Jesse Cox de Porres, O.P., director of "Sign Me Up!"—a special project for evangelization in the inner city of the Detroit Archdiocese—asked if I would like to apply for a job with the program. That was truly a blessing. Not only was it a steady job, but something I supported wholeheartedly. The program was designed to encourage the seventeen parishes of the then "hub vicariate" in the inner city of Detroit. It was an evangelistic outreach of the archdiocese that sought to engage Catholics in evangelization by going out into the community, knocking on doors, and inviting people to come to church. It was a dynamic way to make our presence as Catholics felt in the communities. Catholics have largely moved out of most of these communities in Detroit, leaving just a small number to occupy the pews of these big beautiful churches. We know that there are many people in these communities who don't have any faith at all but would love to become Catholic if only they were invited. Our job is to invite them.

In 2003, we went to 665 homes and had twenty-nine responses. In 2004, Sign Me Up! touched well over 3,000 homes. Once we bring these people to their local parishes, it is then the job of the parish to be prepared to receive these people and to catechize them properly. Some of the people we reached were ex-Catholics. Some were lapsed

Catholics who hadn't been to church in more than twenty years. Some had been hurt, and no one had ever reached out to them. Suddenly, we appeared on their doorstep and encouraged them to think about coming home. For some, that's all they needed to begin the process. It is a small start, but it is a start. And we just keep on working. In order to build up these inner-city parishes, we also need full pastoral support and cooperation, so we work with the people of the parish, particularly those involved with adult education, RCIA, and catechesis.

One of the things I find very critical to the evangelization process is the community to which the evangelized person comes. It is the community that causes people to stay in that particular parish. People look for community. The community of parishioners needs to break the tradition and habit of simply coming to Mass, receiving Communion, singing the traditional hymns, and then going home. The parishioners need to get involved in evangelization by going through an inner conversion and demonstrating that conversion by working together in the parish. There is a need to build a warm, loving parish. A parish that is on fire—really reaching out and making new members feel welcome—is a parish people will come back to.

As Catholics, we have so much to offer, but we don't always offer it or even know how to offer it. So many Catholics, as well as Protestant denominations, are tied into a comfort zone they don't want to come out of. That's much of what we found at Saint Suzanne's. There was an unwillingness to accommodate our African-American heritage in any way, shape, or form. We understood why, but still, it made it very difficult for many of my people.

It is nearly impossible for African Americans in this country to come into the Catholic Church unless they are willing to accept a "Euro-style" worship—and few are. There are masses of African Americans who would really benefit from the Lord's Table, but they will not tolerate a "Euro-style" worship. It does not reflect their face—something which it must do. Most African Americans don't have an appreciation of an age-old liturgy. It is dead to them. They want something that speaks to them. This is one of my biggest challenges. I would like to see more African Americans coming into the Catholic Church. This is the fulfillment of the Christian faith, and I know if they knew what I now know, they would be flooding the Church and tearing down the doors.

Africa is exploding with conversions. When I was invited to Uganda, East Africa, in 2003, to participate in a revival, I was awed and inspired by the reverent, yet Spirit-filled worship of the African Catholics. The Church in America must enculturate. Does that mean all churches should become like that? Absolutely not. But I think Pope John Paul II and many of the Vatican Fathers have been correct in saying that the Church has to adapt so that she reflects the face of the culture she is part of. In Europe you have "Euro-style" worship that is thousands of years old, and that is great. But as the Church grows in nations like Africa and the Arabic countries, she must reflect those cultures. That gives the Church true diversity and, at the same time, true unity. It is the same Mass, but the songs and the language and the mannerisms must reflect that particular culture.

My work with Sign Me Up! is right up my alley, and it has been a blessing for me to be part of a tremendous team of people working toward evangelization and enculturization within the parishes. Near the end of 2004, I was asked to take on the position of director of Sign Me Up! when Fr. Jesse announced he was going on sabbatical. Being so new to the Church, I spent considerable time in prayer before agreeing to become director for a year.

In the meantime, I continue to take classes at Sacred Heart Major Seminary. I started there in September of 2000 while participating in RCIA at Saint Suzanne's. My son Joseph started the following semester, and both of us continue our education in theology and philosophy. By the fall of 2002, I decided to apply for the diaconate. My spiritual advisor, Father Dan Trapp, encouraged me in that direction. As a deacon, I knew I would be able to serve at the Lord's Table and to preach. But the overriding reason I wanted to become a deacon was to serve. This is an excellent opportunity to serve Christ and be the hands of the Church and the hands of the bishop.

I was accepted for the diaconate program in May 2003. Because of my background and because of the classes I had already taken, I was moved ahead three years in the program and was able to begin my diaconate internship at Saint John Neumann Catholic Church in Canton, Michigan, during Advent 2004. I have been privileged to serve under the direction of Deacon Pat Conlen and Father George Williams, one of the archdiocese's African-American priests, in this suburban parish of nearly 3,900 families.

On a warm sunny Saturday, October 1, 2005, along with Jene Wesley Baughman, Michael David Chesley and Michael Alan Somervell, I was ordained to the permanent diaconate of the Archdiocese of Detroit by Cardinal Adam Maida at the Cathedral of the Most Blessed Sacrament in Detroit, Michigan.

During the ceremony, my thoughts centered on the blessedness of receiving apostolic ministry. I wept as we lay prostrate before the altar—how favored of God I must be to receive such a gift!

The ordination has changed my perspective of who I am and the work I am called to do. Having received such a blessed gift, I must now be on guard to say or do nothing that will tarnish the grace I have received. I sincerely want to do the work of a deacon; I want to serve God's people and the community at large. I have no interest in celebrity status because I have been called and sealed to serve. The greatest work that I will do will never be seen by the public.

I was assigned to serve at Saint Mary of Redford, Saint Suzanne/Our Lady Gate of Heaven (my home parish) and St. Thomas Aquinas parishes, all in Detroit.

My greatest desire as a deacon is to serve the poor. I want to serve those who are hurting, to be the hands of Christ. As I try to discern the will of God, I am certain that this is pleasing to him—to take on the complete self-lessness he demonstrated when he became one of us, that complete abandonment of self in service to others—to feel the pain of others and to reach out to others.

That is what I want. Still, I know that it's not what *I* want that matters, it's what *he* wants. So I continue to pray to do his will. For now, the calls are still coming to speak across the United States and in other countries. Sometimes I get three calls a day to speak at churches, revivals, and conferences. People have told me I have given them hope, a reason and encouragement to come into the Church or not to leave the Church. I see a great hunger out there for knowledge of the Catholic faith. People want to know their faith, really know it. I feel humbled that God has chosen me to be an instrument to bring encouragement to his people.

My ministry before becoming Catholic was good. It worked and it blessed people. It was a gift from God, but he asked me to give it back, and I did. He molded it, changed it, and gave it back to me, but what he has given me now stupefies me. I can't even begin to comprehend it. It just amazes me the effect it has on others. But I know that it is not me, and that's what makes it so humbling—when you know that it is not you at all, that God is using you. He has created a totally new ministry that is completely his, not mine. He gets all the credit. I just say yes, show up, and am always completely amazed by what he does. Before I go out and speak, I always talk to God and say: "Please don't let me get too familiar with this. I always need you to be there for your people. Please don't let my sins affect what I say to your people." Then I have no fear and no doubts. I very seldom use notes, and when I stand up to speak, it just comes to me what to say. I know that's his gift.

Although I will most likely stay in school for the rest of my life because I love learning, I will never be a scholar. What I am is a witness, and I am encouraged by Pope Paul VI's apostolic exhortation, *Evangelii Nuntiandi*. He says that this generation needs witnesses and listens to witnesses more so even than teachers unless the teachers are also witnesses— witnesses of holiness through God's grace.[1]

---

[1] "Without repeating everything that we have already mentioned, it is appropriate first of all to emphasize the following point: for the Church, the first means of evangelization is the witness of an authentically Christian life, given over to God in a communion that nothing should destroy and at the same time given to one's neighbor with limitless zeal. As we said recently to a group of lay people, 'Modern man listens more willingly to witnesses than to teachers, and if he does listen to teachers, it is because they are witnesses.' ... St. Peter expressed this well when he held up the example of a reverent and chaste life that wins over even without a word those who refuse to obey the word.... It is therefore primarily by her conduct and by her life that the Church will evangelize the world, in other words, by her living witness of fidelity to the Lord Jesus—the witness of poverty and detachment, of freedom in the face of the powers of this world, in short, the witness of sanctity" (Pope Paul VI, *Evangelii Nuntiandi*, Apostolic Exhortation, paragraph 41).

So I tell those to whom I speak: I don't come to you as a teacher. Your priest and your bishops are your teachers. I come to you as a witness of God's grace—what God can do; what he has done for me and what I know he will do for you. I am a witness of God's grace—no more and no less.

I am so awed by what God has done in my life. All I can do is simply and humbly follow.

Why me?

Why not me?

I sought the truth, and God, in his great mercy, did not disappoint me. Our God is a "weak" God (see 1 Cor 1:25) in that he cannot say no to those who call upon him in love and faith, just as in the story of the Canaanite woman.

> And behold, a Canaanite woman from that region came out and cried, "Have mercy on me, O Lord, Son of David; my daughter is severely possessed by a demon." But he did not answer her a word. And his disciples came and begged him, saying, "Send her away, for she is crying after us." He answered, "I was sent only to the lost sheep of the house of Israel." But she came and knelt before him, saying, "Lord, help me." And he answered, "It is not fair to take the children's bread and throw it to the dogs." She said, "Yes, Lord, yet even the dogs eat the crumbs that fall from their masters' table." Then Jesus answered her, "O woman, great is your faith! Be it done for you as you desire." And her daughter was healed instantly (Mt 15:22–28).

His love is breathtaking—not that he doesn't discipline or correct us—but he ultimately desires for us to be in union with him.

My ministry now is the Lord's doing, so I take no credit for any of it. He opens doors and says: Go here. And I go. He says: Say this. And I say it. I go day to day wherever the Lord leads me, and I am totally in awe.

15

Reflections

If I knew when I was younger what I know now, I believe I would have become a priest. But I didn't know. And God had other plans for me.

I had a wonderful early life as a Christian in the Pentecostal church. I think about that sometimes, and it brings tears to my eyes. I think about those times with those dear people and what a wonderful time we had serving the Lord. We just loved the Lord, and we loved one another. It was a small, close-knit community, and our lives revolved around worshipping God and doing good, and we loved it. The young people grew up together, and our greatest joy was in doing good. A virtuous life was the life we loved to live. We loved prayer, and we loved worship, and we loved coming together at potlucks and sharing our experiences with one another. We loved talking about the Bible and arguing different points of view. It was so exhilarating. Our lives centered around living, rejoicing, praying, fasting, digging out Scriptures, and debating the fine points of law and Gospel and grace. I loved it. I still do love it.

But now I see that all of what I had before may have seemed perfect, but it was not complete. Now I understand that God's working is far greater than I ever thought—it is incomprehensible. What I have now is an amazing continuation of those wonderful early days. I had gone to the limit of those early days. Now that limit has been taken off, and there is a limitless growth in the things of God.

Before it was like swimming in a wonderful twenty-five-foot-deep river, lined with beautiful trees. Somehow, by God's grace, I reached the mouth of that river and found the ocean, the bottomless ocean with the sun on the horizon, and it is beyond comprehension. It is limitless.

I do miss many of the old expressions, the methods of worship, the freedom, the music, and the preaching—especially the preaching. I have found nothing in the Catholic Church that quite parallels the freedom, the joy, and the power of a good Pentecostal worship service. But the thing that sets the Catholic Church apart from all other churches is the Eucharist, the presence of our Lord Jesus Christ in the Eucharist. In other churches, the presence and power of the Holy Spirit is there; the joy of the Lord is there; but the Eucharist is not there. That is the center of worship in the Catholic Church and has been so for two thousand years.

I do miss the things of my former life because they are still a part of me, but I can't disregard the truths I've learned. I could never go back! It is like reminiscing about high school days in your forties: you have warm feelings about the experiences and relationships that you once enjoyed, but life has matured far beyond those adolescent days. I cannot repudiate my religious past. My spiritual life began in the Pentecostal fires of the Church of God in Christ, later grew to incorporate the dynamism and scripturally oriented teachings of Evangelical Christianity, and has finally found its completion in the liturgy and life of the Catholic Church. And what keeps me here is the knowledge that this *is* the Church of the New Testament! This is the Church in which I have found the legacy of the apostles, the martyrs, the saints (especially Mary, the Mother of God), and two thousand years of doctrinal development.

And, finally, it is here that I find the True Presence in the Eucharist.

Of course with every paradigm shift there are a whole new set of negatives, and there are many negatives within the Catholic Church. The Church is holy, but the faithful are in the process of living out their call to holiness. Consequently, one finds imperfect people with hidden agendas or imperfect people struggling with racism, duplicity, immorality, injustice, hypocrisy, spiritual lethargy, outlandish religious perspectives or superstition, and the usual list of human failings. But as a former pastor of two congregations, I know that all who work in any human endeavor encounter the same human failings! Just because the Catholic Church is the Church of the Upper Room does not exempt her from harboring in her bosom sinners who need the healing grace of a loving God.

For many of the people that came with me into the Church, it has been a struggle adapting to the primarily Anglo-Saxon type of worship. It wasn't so difficult for me because I had more of an understanding of the faith and had spent many years in study. But for those that didn't have the same depth of understanding, it was a big struggle, especially for the first couple of years. Even now, there is some struggle. They miss that spontaneity and celebratory aspect of worship. Yet time has a way of healing and bringing about change. Slowly many of them are beginning to understand and fall in love with the Church and her liturgy.

Very recently, my sister Gwen, who was prepared to walk away from me at one point, told me, "I love being Catholic! I love everything about it! I see it very clearly now, and I just love being Catholic!"

Unfortunately, a few of the people, who initially came into the Church, have left to go back to Protestant denominations. Some have changed parishes and are attending predominantly African-American Catholic churches in Detroit.

And there are those that did not follow me into the Church. In December 2003, about forty-five former members of Maranatha met at a restaurant with me. They were glad to see me, and we enjoyed one another's company. Some had questions for me. They wanted to know what was going on in my life.

One of the young women there had been like a daughter to me and is grown now. She is a member of a very strict Evangelical church that is extremely anti-Catholic. I asked her if she was seeking the truth, and she said she was. But she didn't like it when I told her that she would find it in the most unlikely places. These former Maranatha members and I are keeping the dialogue going and plan to meet at least annually.

So I remain open to whatever the Lord wants me to do and whomever the Lord wants me to touch with his message. I'm just happy to be in his Church and in the fullness of the faith.

This is the Church. This is the hierarchy and the foundation Jesus left for us. This is the authority he gave. And to be a part of that structure means more than anything. Just to know that I'm in the Church of the Upper Room is sufficient. Everything else is simply icing on the cake.

I love this faith with all its warts and moles. I love it because it is the Church of Jesus Christ.

Photo 20. Donna with her sponsor Janet Ray.

Photo 21. Alex and Donna as they processed into the church.

Photo 22. The Jones' granddaughter, Lauren Jones, was born during the time of RCIA classes and had already been received into the Church through baptism—the first "cradle" Catholic in the Jones family.

Photo 23. The Jones family at the altar of Saint Suzanne's.

Photo 24. Alex is confirmed by Father Dennis Duggan, as a smiling Dennis Walters keeps his hand firmly on Alex' shoulder.

Photo 25. Sponsor Janet Ray places her hand on Donna's shoulder during confirmation. The Jones' granddaugher, Camille Jones (left), awaits her turn.

Photo 26. Alex receives his First Holy Communion on his knees.

Photo 27. Alex receives the Precious Blood from sponsor Dennis Walters.

Photo 28. A time of profound reflection follows the Jones'
First Holy Communion.

Photo 29. Alex with Father George Williams, pastor of Saint
John Neumann Church, Canton, Michigan,
speaking with parishioners after giving a talk in
March 2004 about his conversion story. Alex was
later assigned to that parish for his deacon internship, beginning during Advent of that year.

Photo 30. Alex feels humbled that God has chosen him to
serve as a witness to the Catholic faith. The Saint
John Neumann Church presentation (where this
photo was taken) was just one of many given by
Alex across the United States and in numerous
countries.

PART TWO

DONNA'S STORY

I

Purely Pentecostal

Life takes us through many twists and turns, and it is an understatement to say that my life is no different. Many times as I sit in my prayer room at home, and gaze at the icons of Mother Mary and her Son, Jesus, I want to pinch myself just to be sure that my entrance into the Catholic Church was real. To me, it is nothing short of miraculous because I can now see clearly how God himself choreographed the events of my life that brought me home to his Church.

Let me give you a glimpse of my background. My fraternal twin, Dianne, and I were born in Chicago, Illinois. At the age of two-and-a-half, we were placed in a wonderful foster home with Bernice and Francis Myers who had a little girl, Debbie, just a year younger than Dianne and me. Our foster parents soon came to love us as their own. Even though we were never officially adopted by them, we lived with my foster mom until we both married. I find it quite ironic now that my foster mom was Pentecostal and my foster dad was Catholic.

My earliest memory of church was going to Sunday school at a house church with Elder Tucker as the pastor. Mom would get us girls ready and send us off to church, and she would come later. My dad seldom accompanied us to church, but attended services at a local Catholic church. I recall two occasions in particular that gave me a child's perspective of what went on in the Catholic Church. But because no one explained these experiences to me and since I had no frame of reference, I was unable to make sense of the things I saw. My first experience of the Catholic Church was attending a funeral Mass with my dad. It seemed more like a mausoleum than a church to me. It was large, dark, damp, and cold. Everyone dressed in drab colors. I remember water being flung all over the place, and I didn't like it at all. The second occasion was attending vacation Bible school when we lived in Bangor, Michigan.

Dianne and I moved with our family to a beautiful, ranch-style home in Gary, Indiana. We were there only a short time before our parents began experiencing marital problems. By the time a year had passed, they had decided to divorce, but for the sake of us children, they remained on friendly terms. As a single mom, our mother provided for us by substitute teaching during the winter and working as a maid at a resort during the summer. Although it was not an easy time, Mom made it look that way.

The money Mom received as part of her divorce settlement afforded her an opportunity, along with members of her family, to purchase a farm in Bangor, Michigan. This is where we spent our summers. We would close up our house in Gary and become a country family for several months after school was out. There was a different atmosphere in the farming community and an entirely different code of ethics. Caucasians and African Americans lived easily side by side, unusual during that time. I believe God was training me in my youth to see people as individuals and not to judge them by the color of their skin. He was preparing me for his Church—comprised of all nationalities and races.

Our summers were filled with country air and farm chores like gathering dropped apples after commercial pickers had visited neighboring orchards. Our mother would wrap each apple individually in newspaper for storage through the winter. Our own property was framed with walnut trees, so in the fall we would pick up the walnuts and crack the skins surrounding them. They were still considered green, so we would put them in a brown feed sack to dry out. Then, in the winter, we would crack the shells and eat them by the potbellied stove. Later we sold the house in Gary and moved to the farm permanently.

When Mom first purchased the farm, the house was still being renovated and had no running water. There was an outside pump, and we had to pump the water and heat it up on the stove in order to wash dishes and clean the house. It wasn't long, though, before our farm home had the same modern conveniences as our home in Gary. But the farm required an entirely different set of responsibilities than city living. On the farm, I had the outside chores in the morning, and I would get up and milk the cow, tie the goat outside, and feed the chickens, then catch the bus for school at eight o'clock. When we came home, we put on our straw hats and had chores to do before supper and homework. All our friends lived similar lives, so we didn't feel any different.

Mom was an amazing woman and would work from eight o'clock in the morning to five in the evening as a maid at a nearby resort in the summertime. We three girls would get together and divide up the housework and the chores so Mom would not have so much to do when she came home in the evening. Many times, by the end of the day, our mother's feet were swollen twice their normal size. She would rest a short time then begin her own chores like washing the second-hand jars she had purchased from the Goodwill store for canning the late summer produce.

Mom was also quite an entrepreneur. She and my grandmother started a convalescent home. They recognized the desire of many families of seniors to find a homelike atmosphere for their loved ones, and so they set up their business like a small family home to accommodate that desire. They started out with just three residents and eventually added a second small home.

This venture gave my mother and family a certain amount of financial independence. Mom could afford to give us the things we needed and some of the things we wanted, but she also expected us to work for some of those things we desired. We were expected to earn money to buy our school clothes in the fall. That meant summertime was a time for us to work in the berry fields. In Bangor, rich or poor, the children worked in the blueberry fields for their summer employment. We would work side-by-side with our friends from school. Mom also encouraged our own sense of entrepreneurial adventure. When our own crop of vegetables matured, she would set up a fruit and vegetable stand in front of our house so we could sell our goods to passersby.

Summer vacation was not meant to be a vacation from God, and Mom often sent us to vacation Bible school. One year, oddly enough, she sent us to a local Catholic church where the activity was held. There I met a little Caucasian girl who served, to the best of her ability, as my personal Catholic guide, explaining various things and answering my questions. As I had years earlier at my dad's church, I wondered about the men in long black robes and white collars and the women also in long black robes and headgear accented with white. My friend explained that the men were priests and were called "Father", and the women were nuns and were called "Sister". She was so sincere in her respect for them that I began to see them through her eyes as very special individuals.

One day she told me she had done something wrong and needed to go to confession. I went with her into the church where she went into this tiny room, no bigger than a phone booth. It had a red curtain that went all the way to the floor covering the doorway. I sat down and waited until she came out of the little room. She explained to me that she had told the "Father" what she had done wrong, and he told her to say ten to fifteen Hail Marys. She added that doing this would make up for what she had done wrong. It all sounded a little strange to me, so when I went home I told my mother what had happened. She simply said they did those things because they were Catholic, then she took me out of that vacation Bible school. That gave me the impression, since Mom would send us to other non-Catholic Bible schools, that those Catholics must be spiritually on the wrong track.

My mother always was, and still is, a devout Christian. Although she went through a difficult time during the divorce, she showed us how to live a life that would be pleasing to God. She used her God-given gifts to the best of her ability and, with all of her heart, she said Yes to God. Later, as I began to make my journey into the Catholic Church, memories of her example would help me. I can truly say that my mother had an unquenchable thirst and sincere desire to know what plan God had for her life. Her desire compelled her to keep company with the holy women in her church who dedicated themselves to prayer. Women like Mother Boyd, Mother Williams, and Mother Hines were regular visitors to our house. My mother's sister, whom we called "Tea", was Mom's daily prayer partner. These holy women of God would sometimes stay for three or four days with us. They would fast, and I would see them lying prostrate, praying on the living room floor.

Mother Estella Boyd was one of my favorite people who visited us on the farm. She and my mother were great friends, and she would sometimes stay with us on the farm for several weeks. Her daughters were close to our ages, so we would have playmates during their stay. Mother Boyd was very reverent, charismatic, honest, and open. While she was with us, we would often gather around the potbellied stove in the evening and listen to her speak about the goodness of God and the great things she had seen God do in her life. She would often kneel by the stove and pray. Being an early riser, I would sometimes find her at four or five in the morning, praying by the stove. By that time the fire had gone out, and the air in the house would be so cold that you could see your breath, so I would put another quilt on her.

Mother Boyd's dedication to God was inspiring, and I wanted to do all I could to make her comfortable. I would bring her whatever she needed, and she started calling me her nurse. Her life was one of virtue and, looking back now, reminds me in some ways of the lives of the saints. Little did I know then that this godly woman would be instrumental in introducing me to my husband.

My mother was also a truly moral and godly woman and a wonderful example for her daughters in word and deed. She always started her day with prayer and Bible reading. She would pray with us before we left for school or went about our business for the day. Mom's favorite saying was, "With God first and education second, there is nothing that you can't achieve."

Mom began a practice, from the time we were young, of sitting us down on Saturdays and teaching us about life. She told us that she wanted to prepare us to be able to live in the White House and dine with the president if the opportunity presented itself. Mom wanted her girls to be well-rounded, so she also exposed us to concerts, the library, the art museum, and other places that were of educational interest. She felt that children should explore their interests and that it was most effective when done with family members taking the time out of their schedules to introduce the children to wholesome activities and cultural treasures.

She gave us a mental moral measuring stick for choosing our friends, selecting a mate, and conducting ourselves as married women when that time arrived. She taught us how to pray to God about the things going on in our lives and helped us to understand that God is concerned even about the little needs of his children. While there were times I would rather be playing than learning about God and life lessons, her teaching proved very valuable in years to come, and I will be forever grateful to her for all the time and love she invested in us. She taught us to be chaste and virtuous so that we would grow to be godly women. She would tell us that God has godly men just like he has godly women, and, if we lived godly lives, God would send us husbands after his own heart. Years later, after I married and moved 180 miles from where my mother and stepdad lived (my mom had remarried by then), her lessons were just like a record playing—I could hear her teachings, and all I had to do was to apply them to each situation. They proved invaluable as Alex and I raised our family and continued our education.

Even though Mom was Pentecostal, she was bold in her exploration of other denominations. During my youth, Mom's brother was ill, and she sought God's healing for him. She wasn't afraid of investigating other denominations for that purpose. Mom would bring my uncle and grandmother along with us and would put pillows and blankets in the back of the car for us girls to sleep on as we made late-night trips back from visiting other churches and revivals. We covered the evangelical circuit, worshipping in tent revivals with the likes of Oral Roberts, A. A. Allen, Rev. Freeman, and Brother Branan, to name a few. We worshipped with a wide selection of denominations, except Episcopal, Lutheran, and Presbyterians. And, of course, we would have nothing to do with the Catholics by that point.

That had not always been the case. There had been times during those early years when Mom and Dad made some attempts at reconciliation. During that time, Mom would take us with her to Chicago and to the Catholic church my dad attended there. Perhaps because I was still feeling hurt that my dad had left Mom, I remember having an abrasive attitude whenever I walked into the Catholic church. It just rubbed me the wrong way. I was angry, and I wanted nothing to do with my dad's church. Mom was still angry too, and her anger showed in her conversation and remarks about the Catholic Church. Still, as I look back on all this, I believe that God was preparing me, through Mom's example of fearlessness in seeking God, always to seek the truth of God's Word no matter where it would lead me. This seeking, of course, eventually led me to enter Christ's Church—the Catholic Church.

2

A Godly Man for a Godly Woman

Looking back now, I am amazed at how well Mom prepared me to be a pastor's wife. Since we lived about thirty miles from the nearest Pentecostal church, my mother took some of the money she received in the divorce settlement and had a small church built on our property. She was eager to do whatever she could to worship God and to expose others to God. Every Saturday she would send us girls down to clean the church. We would complain sometimes and ask why we had to clean the church *every* Saturday. She would tell us, "If you are faithful in the little things, God will make you ruler over many."

When the church was finished, Mom and my aunt would go there and pray that God would send them a pastor for the church. He sent many preachers that came and went. My mother told them they could take the money from the collection to pay for their services of ministering the Word to the people, but to leave some to pay for the oil we would need to heat the church in the wintertime. Well, winters would come, and there would not be enough money for the oil. It wasn't long before I realized some of these men of God were not properly handling the monies they were put in charge of. I became thoroughly disgusted with them when I realized they had used their gift only for gain and had not displayed a godly character. I made up my mind then that I wanted nothing to do with them or anyone that acted like them. I decided I definitely would never want a preacher for a husband—I would rather have an unsaved businessman than a sanctified preacher!

One summer, my mom surprised us when she said she was taking us on vacation back to Gary, Indiana. We didn't normally take vacations, so I was just a little suspicious. My suspicions were confirmed when we arrived at my aunt's home in Gary. I learned that my aunt wanted to introduce me to a Baptist preacher, and my mom informed me that Mother Boyd had a teacher she wanted me to meet as well.

I thought, "Mmm, hmm!" I could see that my mother, aunt, and Mother Boyd were all playing cupid. I had already made up my mind that I wasn't going to be interested in these young men. I was absolutely determined not to get involved with a preacher and, for all I knew, that teacher could be a preacher too.

It turned out that my auntie wanted to hook me up with a Baptist preacher because she wanted him to get saved, and, of course, she didn't believe the Baptists were saved. But Mother Boyd introduced me to Alex Jones, saying, "This is the teacher I wanted you to meet."

I said, "*School* teacher? He's not a preacher? Okay, we're in business."

Alex and I began dating soon after meeting, but I was so chaperoned it wasn't funny! Alex would teach school all day in Detroit and then get in the car and drive 180 miles one way to visit with me for two hours. Later, when Alex' friend, Larry Mann, began dating my twin sister, Dianne, both of them would visit at the same time and take turns driving. Alex and I had to sit in the living room while my stepfather sat in the dining room, pretending he was reading the Bible with his magnifying glass when he was actually watching us and listening to what we were saying. It didn't matter. I knew I had found just the type of man I was looking for in a husband. Alex was a mature and godly man.

As it turned out, Dianne and I, born on the same day, later shared the same wedding day, although we were married in two different Michigan cities. Alex and I moved to our first apartment after we were married.

After nearly a year I discovered I was pregnant with our first child, so we moved into a larger four-family flat that belonged to Alex' aunt in Detroit. Living in a big city was far, far different than living in Gary and light years away from the sheltered life we had lived on the farm. Alex came home one day to find that I had the back door open. Concerned for my safety, he was very upset, but on the farm we had always felt safe and had left our doors open and unlocked. It was a different world in Detroit. There was wire over the windows, and it seemed more like jail to me. I could look out from my apartment on Seward Street and see the pimps working their areas on Twelfth Street dressed in their wide hats, chartreuse shirts, and platform shoes. Their ladies of the evening were working the streets with them. They never bothered anyone outside of their area of operation. My thought was, "Well, that's their life, and this is mine."

Once when I was talking to my mom on the phone as I gazed out our window, I saw a man snatch a woman's purse and run down the alley. A policeman came running after him but didn't see which way he went, so I yelled, "He went that-a-way, sir!" My mother was startled and concerned about my well-being. I can now see that God has always watched over me and protected me and my family. We moved away from Twelfth Street into a more stable neighborhood when our two oldest boys were under the age of two. On the block where we lived there were two-parent families. Still, in that neighborhood there were many families without a father in the home, and many ways for young boys to get into trouble. We were kind of like the Cosbys with our structured family life and emphasis on church and morals. Still, that didn't prevent our boys from getting involved in some very difficult situations.

One day, Alex caught me completely off guard when he came home and told me he felt that God was calling him to preach. I felt the Lord had tricked me—he waited until after we were married, and then called Alex to be a preacher! I reminded God that I didn't want to be married to a preacher. But I knew that Alex was answering God's call. I had often seen him spend hours studying the Bible and other books in order to gain a better understanding of the Word of God. I was subtly reminded that God has a sense of humor, and it was, after all, not my will, but his that would be done.

Money was tight at that time, however; so I took on an afternoon job and started back to school. As a family, we would attend church, and the pastor would occasionally allow Alex to preach on a weeknight. Alex was also involved in Fellowship, a ministry cofounded by Mother Boyd. He would work long hours after teaching all day, trying to build this ministry. God was preparing me, though I didn't realize it at the time, for the responsibility of serving as a pastor's wife. Meanwhile, I was the one doing the preaching at home to our children during the week. God gave me the wisdom to impart the Word to them: Do unto others; don't lie; don't cheat; don't steal. Alex and I set the rules, but I was generally the enforcer.

Then Alex took on the awesome responsibility of pastoring at Zion Congregational Church of God in Christ in Detroit. He would come home from teaching all day, eat, take a nap, and then go back to the church in the evening. The boys really didn't see too much of their father until the weekends, when he would play with them and do the dad thing.

Attending college, taking on a new role as the pastor's wife, and trying to keep up with three little boys seemed daunting at times. Fortunately, I had a mentor, Gloria, who was "street-wise". I believe God gave this woman the gift of wisdom. She would counsel me about many things concerning the natural attitudes of people and how to deal with them. While her advice was very helpful, I needed someone to turn to for advice on how to be a pastor's wife, someone to serve as a mentor in this new role. But I had no one to turn to at the time—no support group of pastors' wives, not even one. It seemed I had so many new responsibilities all at once. Then during one of the evening services, the Spirit of God overshadowed me. He instructed me to stop going to college and to be a support to my husband and a fulltime mother to my boys. It was the best move I could have made. God continued to teach me, during times of prayer, how to help my husband serve the congregation. The bonding that subsequently occurred during that time was priceless.

As a fulltime mom, I was also the disciplinarian during the week. The boys knew they had to be home and sitting on the porch before sundown. If they weren't there, they knew I would be chasing them home, and they also knew I could outrun them—I had run track when I was in high school. Alex and I kept a tight watch over the boys until they were about sixteen and began to venture out more. When the two oldest were high-school-aged, we enrolled them in Notre Dame Catholic. We knew it was a good Christian school with an excellent academic foundation. Unlike some of the Detroit public schools, it was safe, and the parent involvement was amazing. Looking back now, God's plan is so clear. He guided us in placing two of the boys in a Catholic school and giving them a basic understanding of the faith—something that helped immensely as we prepared them to enter the Church years later. Our oldest, Joseph, graduated from Notre Dame. Benjamin, on the other hand, didn't like the all-boys environment. "Ma," he would complain to me, "I get tired of looking at mustaches." He transferred to Pershing, a public high school, in eleventh grade. He had such a good background from Notre Dame that he was in honors English and math at Pershing. Marc went to Pershing all four years with few problems.

It was our middle son, Benjamin, who was more difficult to keep on the straight and narrow. He bonded with some of the boys in the neighborhood who had a negative influence on him. I would just get on my knees and pray. We continued our family nights and prayed together, and I let them know I was putting them in God's hands. I told them, "If you can fight God, you're a big one!" At times, when they were really acting out, I would tell them, "You are hurting my heart." It felt like my heart was twisting inside of me during those times. But God, through his great kindness and mercy, gave my husband and me strength to endure the stressful times we went through with them. The Lord answered my prayers in many ways.

I recall one evening when I was truly frightened about what might happen. Marc (who was the tallest at six feet, but still the baby of the family) was angry with two young men because they had threatened him, and he was out to get revenge. He told his brothers what had happened to him and they were all angry. Our boys started talking and got one another hyped up. They began making phone calls, and I heard, "Hey man, bring me a piece."

Alex wasn't home, and I couldn't reach him, so I just said, "Lord, I don't know what to do!" Within a short time, there were about five or six guys at my house, and they were all carrying weapons. I just got down on my knees and prayed. I recalled the story of Elisha, who was surrounded by an army of Syrian soldiers. Elisha prayed that they would become blind so they wouldn't see him as he walked through the midst of them. God answered Elisha's prayer, and the soldiers did not see him (2 Kings 6:18). Following Elisha's example, I prayed that the Lord would not let my sons and their friends see these two young men they were searching for. I stayed on my knees until I received assurance from the Lord that everything would be all right. An hour later, my sons and their friends came back to the house saying, "Man, I don't understand how someone could just disappear into thin air. Where could they have gone to?"

It turned out that my sons and their armed friends had split up to look for these two boys, but they were nowhere to be seen. I knew that was the Lord. He had answered my prayers. That's what I value more than anything else in the world—this relationship of prayer with the Lord. There is nothing that he can't do. He said, "No weapon that is formed against thee shall prosper" (Is 54:17, KJV).

Another time one of my sons and his friend had words with some other young men. They came with a gun and a bat and went to my son's friend's house first—shooting and kicking in the door. Then they interrogated his mother to try to find out his whereabouts.

Word was out that they were coming to our house next, and I was terrified. The Holy Spirit spoke to my heart and said, "They are not coming near this dwelling." And they didn't. I can't tell you how many times the Holy Spirit would speak to me and tell me that he had a hedge around our house.

The next morning we had to get our boys out of the city because these same thugs were parked in the parking lot on our street waiting to shoot them. My husband made our boys get down in the back seat of the car while he drove them to my sister-in-law Gwen's home in Farmington where they stayed for a couple of weeks until the danger was past.

Trying to raise three boys with a Christian attitude in the middle of the inner city was arduous, to say the least. But since they listened to my husband preach the Word of God every weekend and joined me in prayer time during the week, they had at least heard the Christian message from both of us, and the Lord preserved them until they came into an understanding of their own personal relationship with God.

Even when the boys decided they no longer wanted to attend church, the Lord gave me direction through Alex. I figured if they wouldn't go to church, I was going to bring the church to them. I would give them my five-minute sermon of what their father had said that day. They eventually got to the point where they didn't want to hear it because they were resentful. They didn't want to even see me coming because I was always talking about the Lord. Alex told me to stop preaching to the boys. The Lord directed me just to put them in his hands. He told me to be their mother, to be their friend, and talk about everyday life with them. He basically said to me: *I'll let you know when to talk with them about me. But back off for now and give me a while to work with them. Give me time to show them that I am God in their personal lives.*

And that's exactly what he did.

3

Pastor's Wife

When Alex became pastor at Zion, I felt I was put on a pedestal as the pastor's young wife. But it wasn't long before I began to realize some of the people in the congregation were trying to take me down brick by brick, picking me apart, judging me by my apparel. The Pentecostal church I had been raised in did not teach that wearing such things as sandals, make-up, and jewelry was sinful. This church did. I could have understood the theology that they believed in—if only they themselves had followed it. But when there was a wedding at the church, the very ones doing the finger-pointing would come decked out in style. Yet they would condemn me for matters of my appearance like wearing small earrings. I could do nothing right from their critical viewpoint. So I made up my mind not to appear affected by the judgments, but rather to treat everyone with dignity and respect and to be very approachable no matter what.

The role of a pastor's wife didn't come with a book of instructions, so my philosophy developed over time and through a number of experiences. Other pastors' wives in the same denomination could serve as mentors for a new pastor's wife. Because our church was independent and had its own charter, I was on my own. Plus, the pastor's wife who preceded me had been there for some time and was a more mature woman. This was my husband's first position as a pastor, and I was much younger. I didn't have a good grasp yet on how to respond or how to interact with the members of the congregation. I didn't know whether to respond to them in a formal, impersonal manner or as I would a good friend. Some of the ministers' wives were kind and tried to help, but they weren't pastors' wives. In the Pentecostal church, everyone looks to the pastor's wife to offer comfort, a listening ear, and to represent the church as the first lady of the congregation. As I contemplated my role as pastor's wife, my sister Debbie called me. She was dealing with the same problem from the perspective of a member of her church. She shared with me that she loved her pastor and his wife, but they seemed distant and unapproachable. She wanted to know if this was the proper conduct for people in leadership positions. I told her I didn't know, but would think about it and get back with her.

I thought it would be a good idea to ask the Lord how leaders should conduct themselves with regard to their congregations. It wasn't a prayer, just a thought. It never occurred to me that God is sensitive even to our thoughts, but—thank you, Jesus—he is! So it happened that one day I was on my knees, praying by my bedside, when I felt the presence of Jesus standing right in front of me. I didn't see him, but I knew he was there. His presence went through the bed. He didn't have any restrictions with matter, and his whole being was standing in front of me. He wasn't speaking to me in an audible voice, but rather was intimating to my mind. He revealed to me: *Everything you see I spoke into existence. I hold the hearts of kings in my hand, yet see how easily approachable I am.* Here the Creator of the universe was standing in front of me, answering the question I had in my mind that hadn't even been formulated into a prayer. What a great God we serve! He is so concerned about our every need!

On another occasion, after witnessing the harsh disposition of some leaders in churches in which my husband was a guest speaker, I asked, "Lord, are leaders supposed to be harsh and treat their congregations like children who must blindly follow their directives?"

The Lord intimated to my spirit that pastors and leaders of the church are supposed to show the attributes of Christ to their flocks. They are to be just like the mother and father in the home. The mother and the father set the stage in the home as to how the children will be. If the parents are harsh and domineering, their children will behave that way. If they are aloof and cold, the children will follow in their footsteps. The children are a product of their parents. The leaders are set as examples to the people and should be filled with the presence of God, so they can reflect nothing but Christ to the people. Witnessing that example of Christ in their pastor and church leaders, the members of the congregation, in turn, will interact with one another accordingly. I can truly say that my husband reflected that love of Christ to his congregation.

God helped me to understand that the responsibility of a leader in the church is not to rule like a dictator. Rather, leaders have the responsibility to see the unique qualities of each individual so they can direct them to the area where they can best serve and minister to the Body of Christ. He made it clear that my position was to be a complement to my husband and to be available to show love where needed.

The power of prayer was paramount during my time as the pastor's wife. I prayed for my husband as he ministered to the people.

Alex is an excellent Bible teacher. His preaching had the power to stir people to action and inspire them to move out of their comfort zones and witness the Good News of the Gospel. God has given him many gifts. I have seen him pray for the sick and witnessed God's instant healing through

Alex' ministry. Alex was my husband *and* my pastor, and through his preaching, I received a firm foundation in Christ.

From time to time, Alex would preach a series of talks concerning the errors of many of the churches. He taught that the Episcopal Church was in error, the Lutheran church was in error, the Presbyterian Church was in error, along with many others. It was a given that the Catholic Church was in serious error. Alex pointed out that Catholics worshipped idols and Mary. The Catholic Church had left the track that God had intended. Then God favored and focused on the Pentecostal church. Alex taught this for years. He would periodically bring this back up and reaffirm it all. Looking back on those talks, I realize he was only preaching what he had heard from preachers before him. He was simply repeating what he had been taught through the years.

Zion, the first church Alex pastored, was a well-established church filled with sincere people. Many of them were quite set in their ways; their motto was, "Stay as you started." They were not receptive to the new ideas Alex tried to introduce or the changes he tried to make to promote church growth. There was so much conflict that Alex decided to leave his position in 1982, after eight years at Zion. He felt that the in-fighting would eventually destroy the church and that his leaving would at least keep them together.

The day we said our final good-byes was horrendous. Those who supported him felt betrayed and hurt. Those who didn't were busy spreading gossip and lies about why he was stepping down. Alex wanted to begin his own ministry and build it from the bottom up. He didn't ask anyone to come with him when he left Zion, but some wanted to follow him because they really loved his teaching. Others saw his vision and wanted to help him build his ministry.

He found a building with a small dance hall located in a bad neighborhood, but we didn't care because it represented a fresh start. The hall was transformed into a church, and Alex kept his same grueling schedule of teaching school during the day and pastoring in the evenings and on weekends. Still, I sensed that a weight had been lifted from him. His eyes were filled with excitement instead of exhaustion.

Alex called a meeting with the church members and explained that starting a new ministry was not going to be easy. He wanted them to know they were under no obligation to stay. Many expressed their appreciation to him for the opportunity to help build this new ministry, so Alex began organizing the fledgling church and appointing officers. I believe God was using him in a very powerful way in preaching the Scriptures and serving as an example of holiness. The congregation had twice outgrown the buildings we had purchased, when a Greek Orthodox church building became available. It is not uncommon for some preachers to acquire storefront churches in order to bask in the prestige of being called a pastor, while pocketing the paychecks for their own gain. But Alex loved his ministry and his congregation and was concerned about the future of the children. He wanted them to have a church home long after he retired and was gone.

After making some repairs, Maranatha Christian Church was a vision of beauty, with its polished terrazzo floors and pillars trimmed in gold leaf. It was filled on the day of the dedication in 1986. We were excited about our future there, and Alex had plans to build fellowship with other pastors in the city, to evangelize and to continue preaching and teaching the Word of God. He desired to teach his people that there is a deeper, richer life in Christ that can be found in searching the Scriptures and seeking

God through fasting, prayer, and the gifts God gave the Maranatha community.

Pentecostals are often moved by emotionalism—an excitement of the senses brought on by good music or good preaching. Alex would teach that God is *always* present even though his presence might not be felt through emotions. He would teach that there is no need to announce "the Spirit is here" because the Bible says, "For where two or three are gathered together in my name, there am I in the midst of them" (Mt 18:20). If some got carried away with emotionalism, Alex would stop it. He preached that God is calling people to allow him to infiltrate their lives with his Spirit, which comes through obeying God's Word. This infiltration of the Spirit would be reflected in the way people lived their lives. But there were those who didn't understand or didn't appreciate what my husband was trying to do and teach. Still, Alex remained determined to stay pure to the instructions God had given him. His greatest desire was to teach the Word of God properly and to hold fast to it no matter what the cost to him personally.

As the pastor's wife, the first stage of my Maranatha experience was to work with troubled women. I felt ill-equipped and unprepared, but God prepared me. These were hurting women, and some were on drugs. I didn't know what to say at first since I had not been educated in this area. But God assured me; you pray and I'll give you the words—I'll teach you what to say. And he did. It's marvelous when you can be an instrument of God. He equipped me, giving me the skills I needed while I was on my knees. He led me to books I needed to help me be a more effective counselor. As a mother, God gave me the words to say while praying with our sons during their times of stress and trouble. And as a counselor, he did the same while I prayed with these troubled women.

God often taught me spiritual lessons through everyday situations. Many times I would share these lessons with the individual I was counseling at the time. One important lesson I learned took place while I was in the kitchen preparing to fry chicken. I had just put a mound of shortening, resembling an iceberg, into a skillet and turned the burner on to melt it. The Lord revealed to me that I must have confidence that the fire would melt the shortening since I had the chicken seasoned and ready to go into the skillet. The Lord was showing me that just as the shortening was being melted from the bottom, a problem is melted in the same way by prayer. You put the problem in God's hands, and God uses the power of prayer to melt that problem down. The problem is not being melted from the top, but from the bottom—the root. Even though you see that block of shortening in the skillet, you're not worried because you know the fire is capable of melting it. Even though the problem seems large, and you can still see the problem as you begin to pray, you have the assurance that the prayer is going to melt that problem from the root when you put it in God's hands. That assurance allows you to be able to go on about your work. The Lord revealed to me that people can often relate to these everyday experiences and stories. In fact, Jesus himself used everyday experiences in his parables in order to illustrate spiritual truths.

For as long as I can remember, Alex always had books and commentaries spread all over the desk. He seemed to consume books one right after another—always seeking the truth. God didn't disappoint him. He favored him by giving him a discerning eye for the truth of the Gospel. Even so, he experienced conflict at both Zion and Maranatha because not everyone fully agreed with what he was teaching. His preaching was powerful because he taught the essentials of holy living. He taught families how to interact. His goal was to develop a community of believers by encouraging them to take the message home as well as outside the church walls and into the community to bring about change. But there were some who wanted to supplant the authority of their pastor. My husband never spoke against them unless they were arguing about doctrinal teaching. Then he would reassure the congregation that those things he was teaching them were true. Surprisingly, many people were not affected by the derogatory things that were said concerning Alex. I believe they recognized that Alex' greatest desire was to discern the Word of God and proclaim it to the whole congregation.

He was also determined not to be a burden to the congregation he so faithfully served. That's why he continued to work as a teacher for so many years. During the summer months, Alex would spend hours at the church serving as a fulltime pastor. His main concern was to be a blessing to the people, yet he was criticized for being a parttime pastor since he returned to teaching school in the fall. When the church was struggling (for a number of years), I would see my husband go with holes in his shoes and put cardboard in the bottom so he could put his pastor's salary back into the church. He was a true servant and a wonderful example for our sons, who saw their father's sacrifice. He wanted to leave a legacy for the children of Maranatha, so we would go without in order to build the community.

Alex always had an unquenchable thirst to know the direction God was leading him, and he finally reached the point where he felt he could not be as effective in his pastoral and administrative duties as long as he was working two

jobs. It eventually became too much for him, so he took an
early retirement from teaching during the twelfth year of
his eighteen at Maranatha. Alex became a far more effective pastor at that time. He had more time to visit the sick
and take care of the needs of his congregation. That's when
the church really started to blossom. God began to stir Alex
to take the church to a higher level. Alex would stay at the
church long hours and pray. God moved through Alex, and
his preaching became even more powerful. He initiated six
o'clock morning prayer on Sundays; eleven o'clock prayer
on Tuesday mornings; and seven o'clock evening prayers on
Thursdays, in addition to the Wednesday night Bible study.

Alex started preaching a series of sermons on the paradigm shift. He stayed on that series of sermons for some
time. He stressed the point of seeing the plan of God and
his purpose from a new perspective. He used the diamond
as an example—how a piece of coal, good only for burn-
ing, could be changed through time and pressure into a
spectacular diamond with a far more glorious purpose.

I recall one Sunday when the power of God was manifested in a compelling way in Alex' preaching. The people
of the congregation were so quiet that you could hear a
pin drop. I and others felt that God was going to do something great in our midst and was giving Alex a higher
anointing.

Alex was a wonderful Bible teacher, and I really enjoyed
the Wednesday night Bible study. He always took the time
to break down the verses of Scripture for us. He would use
the blackboard, slides, and other visual aids to enhance the
lesson he was presenting.

One Friday evening, Alex was very excited when he came
home. He was teaching a series on the First Letter to Timothy and wanted to reenact a service like the disciples had

conducted two thousand years ago. He explained to me some of the details of how the service was conducted in biblical times. He said he would follow the same format, right down to having the men sit on one side of the church and the women on the other. I sarcastically remarked that that should go over quite well! It did sound interesting, but that was one study I was going to miss since I was leaving for a few days to visit my mother and sister Debbie. I told Alex I would look forward to hearing all the details when I returned.

My family visit went well, but when I asked Alex about the Wednesday night service upon my return, he answered, "It didn't go over very well. Mom [Alex' mother] wouldn't even take communion." I could tell he was disappointed.

About a month later, on a beautiful spring day, the paradigm shift God had planned for us began for me. I was resting in my room when I heard the Spirit of the Lord speak to my heart: ". . . and the gates of hell shall not prevail against it." The Lord would often give me passages of Scripture, but not just a portion of a verse. I wondered why he had done that, so I looked it up in Matthew and it read: "And I say also unto thee, That thou art Peter, and upon this rock I will build my church; and the gates of hell shall not prevail against it" (Mt 16:18). I thought about it for awhile then put it on the back burner of my mind with the thought that maybe I was supposed to use it for the women's ministry.

In the days following this experience, Alex seemed to have a foreboding atmosphere surrounding him. He began to separate himself from his normal daily activities. He would fall asleep in the den in front of the television set more times than I care to count. It got to the point where it was about five nights a week. I thought: What is going on with him? He didn't have a restful sleep. I continued to sense a foreboding, almost a demonic presence around him. It was an atmosphere where he was wrestling, fighting, battling something. He was agitated, irritated, and downright grumpy. He seemed to be in turmoil, and I couldn't figure out what was going on. I was distressed by what was happening to him and believed I would need to prepare for spiritual warfare.

Two weeks later, on a beautiful sunny day, we got ready for church and got in the car when Alex announced, "Donna, we're not going to our church today." That wasn't unusual because many times when he got tired and wanted a rest from his daily church duties, he would have one of his deacons take over at Maranatha, and we would go visit another church.

So I said, "Where are we going? Are we going to Pastor Cunningham's church? Are we going to Pastor Wilkins' church? What church are we going to?"

He just answered, "No, we're going to a Greek Orthodox church today."

I instinctively turned and started to ask, "Have you lost your . . ."

Well, wisdom checked me because this man was driving down the highway at seventy miles an hour, and, if he had lost his mind or had had a nervous breakdown, this was not the time to ask him! I decided to wait and pose that question to him when we got back home. But I knew I had a look of shock on my face. I just sank down into my seat and thought, well, they have finally done it. These people at our church who have been opposing him have finally pushed my husband over the edge.

When we reached the Orthodox church, they sat me in the front row, and Alex went back with the priest to observe.

During the service, incense was flying everywhere, and, unfortunately, I'm allergic to incense. It was a nightmare, and I kept saying to myself: When am I going to wake up? I looked at the missal and was trying to decipher what I should read. I was batting at the incense with my right hand and making the sign of the cross with the left. I tried to stay calm, and I tried not to let anyone know that I didn't know what I was doing, but I'm afraid it was painfully obvious.

As the days and weeks went on, I felt like my world was beginning to crumble—as though I was experiencing an emotional earthquake. I was literally shaking. This was my husband. This was my pastor. My whole world was beginning to come apart at the seams. I told myself, "Donna, you've been in some pretty difficult situations before. You know the power of prayer. Get a grip. You must get a grip!" But I felt that I was engaged in spiritual warfare. I believed the devil was trying to switch Alex. He had a spirit of strong delusion overwhelming him. I decided I needed to get the material he was reading in order to counteract the spirit that was overtaking him.

Alex began bringing home stacks of information about the Catholic Church. His table was covered with even more information. He started bringing home piles of books that mounted up on his desk top. At the time, I was taking two classes, leading the women's ministry, plus working fulltime as a loan officer for a mortgage company. Alex' change really disrupted everything in my life. I decided I would pretend to be interested in what he was talking about and use it as an argument to counteract what was happening to him. I needed to get my hands on some of his material in order to use it for ammunition, certainly not for educational information. So I looked on Alex' desk and found a book on the Church Fathers. It was a small book, which was perfect.

With all I had to do, I knew I could handle this one small book. I could gather enough information in order to thwart what was going on in Alex' mind.

What I read took me totally by surprise. I began to read about how Ignatius of Antioch was on his way to Rome to be executed by the lions. He wanted to be bread for the lions, to be the sacrificial cup. My hand began to shake as I put the book back on Alex' desk. I was a Pentecostal, trying to say Yes to God with all my heart. I had done everything I could to support my husband so that the Lord's will would be advanced. Yet, I could feel emptiness and a need to seek God more. There was something missing. When I read Ignatius, I deeply sensed he had something that I did not have. He had the mind to sacrifice his physical body in order to give everything for Christ. I was not at the point of saying: Lion, eat me! I could picture the lion chewing on my arm, and I thought: Not yet!

The next night I read Polycarp. He was an elderly man, and I read how they tried to burn him at the stake and how the fire kept going out. They finally put a spear through him. I thought, "These people have something I do not have. They have a total 'sold-outness' to God that I have not yet reached." I had not yet said Yes to God to that extent. Next I read Clement.

And as I continued to read about the tremendous sacrifices these Church Fathers had made, I was also listening to the television evangelists at night. Soon their words began to seem very superficial to me: "Name it and claim it—God will give you what you want!" It seemed as though I was constantly hearing, "Bless me, bless me, bless me, God!" But here were the Church Fathers asking: What can I give to you, Lord? They were willing to give their very lives. It was such a *tremendous* contrast.

I began to realize that years earlier God had been trying
to give me clues about his Church. Alex had brought home
some reading that included the Maccabees. My first clue
had come in reading about the woman and her seven sons
who refused to disobey God's law by eating swine's flesh as
the King tried to compel them to do. She encouraged each
son not to violate the law of God but to remain faithful to
the one true God. She was forced to watch as each of her
sons was tortured and executed, and I was amazed by their
strength of conviction. She whispered to each of them not
to give in; then she too was executed (2 Mac 7). I asked
Alex why this was not in the Bible, and he answered, "Oh,
those are part of the seven lost books that are not supposed
to be in the Bible." [1]

I knew that the Catholic Church was all over the world
and that it was active in many areas such as hospitals, mis-
sions, and charities. We had been taught by ministers before
Alex that the Catholic Church was the great whore of Babylon (Rev 17:5). When we would pass a Catholic church, I
would mention to Alex that God was certainly blessing the
great whore. And the great whore was certainly providing

---

[1] These books of the Bible, called the Apocrypha or the Deuterocanon-
icals, were included as part of the Septuagint (Greek version of the Old
Testament) but were not in the Hebrew Bible. These books include Tobit,
Judith, 1 and 2 Maccabees, Wisdom of Solomon, Ecclesiasticus (or Sirach),
and Baruch and are found in Catholic Bibles. Catholic Bibles also contain an
additional six chapters (107 verses) in the Book of Esther and another three
chapters (174 verses) in the Book of Daniel. The Septuagint was the "Bible"
of the apostles, and almost all the Church Fathers (with the exception of
Saint Jerome) accepted the Septuagint as the standard form of the Old Testament. During the Protestant Reformation, Protestant leaders such as Luther
removed these books from their Bibles, it appears, for theological rather than
for textual or historical reasons. They opposed such things as prayers for the
dead (Tob 12:12, 2 Mac 12:39–45), intercession of the saints (2 Mac 15:14),
and the intermediary intercession of angels (Tob 12:12, 15).

for her people. I didn't see any other denomination doing what the Catholic Church was doing, especially on such a large scale.

I began to have other flashbacks of different points in my life where, I could now see, God was trying to knock on my door and tell me the Catholic Church is *the* Church. But I was not ready then to consider the possibility that the Catholic Church could possibly be the Church of Jesus Christ.

And I was still not ready.

4

Those Darn Catholics

Meanwhile, before I could fully absorb all I was reading, Alex began making appointments with Catholics he had met, like Steve and Janet Ray and others, to come over and talk with us. I felt they were intruding into our lives. I didn't want them to come, but I didn't know them well enough to tell them to go away. And I certainly didn't want to be rude. After all, this was Alex' home too.

My only concept of what Catholics were like was what I had been exposed to at my stepdad's pre-Vatican II church. My impression was that they were cold, stoic, damp, and indifferent. Then in walked the Rays, both converts to the Catholic Church. Janet seemed very nice and friendly, but quiet. Steve was friendly, warm, effervescing, and exuberant. He was acting more like a Protestant evangelist than like my concept of a Catholic. This seemed to suit Alex just fine. He would have his list of questions, eager to hear Steve's answers. I didn't know what to think. I just knew that I didn't want to be bothered by these people—they were Catholic!

We were invited to the Rays' home for dinner during that summer of 1998, along with Al Kresta, a well-known apologist, Catholic radio talk show host, and "revert" to the Catholic faith; Father Ed Fride, pastor of Christ the King in Ann Arbor, also a convert; and Dennis Walters, RCIA instructor. All were members of Christ the King Parish. There in their midst was my husband asking them what it would take to come into the Catholic Church. I was shocked! All I could think was "What on earth are you talking about?" My Protestant feathers were bristling! I argued with the guests and finally pointed my finger at Al Kresta and shouted, "You shall know the truth, and the truth shall set you free!" Al, to his great credit, didn't say one word. He just got up and went into the kitchen. I was amazed that he didn't get angry or say one harsh word. Stunned, I excused myself and went to the bathroom.

The Holy Spirit seemed angry with me. He intimated to me: *How dare you ridicule and question these people when you haven't researched this yourself? How do you know that what you have been taught is true? You have been taught by ministers who have the love of God in their hearts. They are righteous and holy and preached all that they knew to be true about God, but that does not mean that what they taught was the fullness of truth.*

I felt faint, but still determined to continue the debate if necessary. I came back to the dinner table and asked Dennis Walters if you have to accept Mary as the Mother of the Church in order to be Catholic. He answered yes. That was my Achilles heal. I blurted out, "*I* won't be going into the Catholic Church then!"

When Janet Ray invited me out to lunch to share Catholicism with me, I thought she was making me her project, so I decided I would go along and really test her. I thought, "If this Church is so special, these Catholics should be up on all the graces", so I threw at her every anti-Catholic theological and doctrinal question I could think of. She was very calm and took it all. Other Catholics she had introduced me to seemed intimidated by me. They wouldn't come back. But Janet hung in there and remained calm throughout. If she didn't know the answer, she would say, "Donna, I don't know, but I'll ask Steve and get back with you." And she did. I continued my attempt to provoke her in order to see if this love she seemed to have for me was real. Over and over again, through the following months, she proved it was just that as she continued to deal with me in love.

Everything seemed to be going so quickly. One week we would be at Dr. Riordan's home, and the next he would be at ours. Dialogues continued with the Rays, Dennis Walters, and the Krestas. Meanwhile, I was still going to school and had gone back to work while still directing the women's ministry at church.

We continued visiting Catholic and Greek Orthodox churches, and by the fall of 1999, I felt like a steam engine getting ready to explode. Here I was in the middle of school, work, ministry, and spiritual turmoil, and my husband was acting as though he didn't know whether he wanted to keep his church or not. I didn't know which way he was going, and, worse yet, he didn't seem to know either.

One evening it all came to a head. I was lying in bed watching one of the television evangelists when Alex asked me to come down and watch a video of an Orthodox service. I was livid and refused to come and watch it. I felt this was just one more thing that showed he didn't have any idea what he wanted to do. He certainly wasn't showing me a clear path where he was going.

Then the Holy Spirit nudged me with: "Wives, submit yourselves unto your own husbands, as unto the Lord" (Eph 5:22). Well, now I was angry with God as well as with my husband. I know it's okay to be angry with God because he understands anger, but I didn't want God angry with me for disobeying his voice. I didn't want to get on his bad side, so I yelled to Alex in a very hostile voice, "Oh, all right, I'm coming!"

I smashed back the covers and stormed into the room and plopped down in the chair and started watching the video. I was very critical in my heart of everything I was watching. My husband and I were still debating the idea of going into the Roman Catholic Church. He felt that if this was the Church Christ left on earth he wanted to be a part of it. I still wanted no part of it. I felt there were many things wrong with the Catholic Church and wasn't about to budge.

All of a sudden I felt overshadowed by the Holy Spirit, and the video began to fade into background noise. God was dealing with me about the Roman Catholic Church. He was bringing to the forefront of my mind that this was his Church. He was dealing with me on my general attitude about his Church. He intimated to my heart: *I have taken you through many denominations, yet you managed to maintain a relationship with me. Am I not able to fix whatever is wrong with my Church?* As he spoke those words to me, it was as though he was saying, *It was I who brought you through this; it was I who brought you to this point.* He was announcing to me: *This is my Church. The step that you are reluctant to take is the one I want you to take.* He brought back the Scripture, "... upon this rock I will build my church, and the gates of hell shall not prevail against it" (Mt 16:18). I saw a ravine in front of me. On one side was Protestantism where I stood. On the other was Catholicism. I knew God wanted me to take that leap of faith into the Roman Catholic Church, but I didn't understand Mary, Purgatory, or praying to the saints. I bargained with God that if he wanted me to take that leap of faith, I would do it as long as he would be there to teach me. He intimated to me that if I would make that leap of faith, he would reveal each and every point I had a problem with. All of this took about five minutes. I told God, "Yes! I will take that leap of faith."

I turned to my husband and said, "Alex, I'm Catholic."

Now for months we had spent hours, sometimes until two or three o'clock in the morning, debating Catholic issues. I would frustrate him with my questions and badgering. So I wasn't surprised when Alex just looked at me and said, "Yeah, right!"

He wasn't convinced of my sincerity until I told him to send an email to Steve Ray and tell him that I was, indeed, Catholic.

As soon as I uttered those words, I was concerned about the fellowship of pastors' wives I had started. I thought, "Oh boy, I'm going to have to keep this a secret." I had things to think about and so many questions to deal with. I decided I would tackle my biggest challenge first: understanding the Catholic faith. I knew I would need to reread those issues I had problems with as though I were studying them for the first time. I prayed that the Lord would open my understanding. During the ensuing months, I would walk and talk with God as though I had a physical presence with me. I would carry on conversations with God in the car while I was driving down the road. I'm sure passersby thought I was nuts! But he would respond to me and speak to me in my spirit and lead me to Scripture. God took the Protestant King James version of the Bible to show me the truth of the Catholic Church.

Alex and I had discussions about praying to the saints. He said the saints were like prayer partners. But I asked, "How can you have a prayer partner who's dead?" It still made no sense to me, so I asked God why we should pray to the dead saints. He made it clear to me that they were not dead, but alive in Christ. He directed me to Revelation where the saints make their prayers go up in intercession before God: "After this I beheld, and, lo, a great multitude, which no man could number, of all nations, and kindreds, and people, and tongues, stood before the throne, and before the Lamb, clothed with white robes, and palms in their hands; And cried with a loud voice, saying, Salvation to our God which sitteth upon the throne, and unto the Lamb" (Rev 7:9–10). These folks certainly didn't *sound* dead.

The Lord directed me to another Scripture passage, Luke 9:28–31, where Jesus took Peter, James, and John up to a mountain to pray. As Jesus was praying, his clothes became as bright as a flash of lightning. Then Moses and Elijah appeared in glorious splendor and started talking to Jesus about his leaving Jerusalem, which was an event that was to take place in the future. I realized that if they were talking to him about the future, they certainly knew about the present and could see what was happening at that time! And if they knew about the present and the future, they couldn't be dead! Then the Lord took me to Hebrews 12:1: "Wherefore seeing we also are compassed about with so great a cloud of witnesses, let us lay aside every weight, and the sin which doth easily beset us, and let us run with patience the race that is set before us." The Lord revealed to me that in order to be a witness, these folks had to be aware of what was going on. The saints that have passed on to the next life are viewing what is going on in our lives right now. How much more are they now able to pray for the situations we face!

One day I was washing dishes at the sink and asked the Lord, "What is Purgatory? I was taught you died once for all." He showed me Hebrews 12:22–24: "But ye are come unto mount Sion, and unto the city of the living God, the heavenly Jerusalem, and to an innumerable company of angels, To the general assembly and church of the firstborn, which are written in heaven, and to God the Judge of all, *and to the spirits of just men made perfect*, And to Jesus the mediator of the new covenant, and to the blood of sprinkling, that speaketh better things than that of Abel" (italics added).

God showed me that he was the one who had to make the spirits of just men perfect, and Purgatory was that time and condition necessary to make them perfect. They had been made perfect after they died. I had read these verses many times. It had been right before my eyes. How could I have missed this all these years? I began to wonder how much more I had missed. I was soon to find out.

Meanwhile, Alex was changing our worship service every Sunday so that it looked more and more like a Catholic Mass. Sometimes Alex would have an early meeting on Sunday, so I would come later, and, as I was driving down the highway, I would be praying, "Lord, what are we going to see today? Please, Lord, don't let Alex change the service. Please!" By this time Alex and I were being privately catechized every week by Dennis Walters and were getting a thorough understanding of Catholic teaching, but the others in our congregation were not on the same page. I felt the people were not yet ready for such a profound transformation.

But Alex continued to make changes, and church members would continue to ask me, "Is your husband losing his mind?" This was, after all, my husband! I recall defending him like a lioness to these people, and, at the same time, thinking, "What in the world is he doing?" By this time, I believed the Catholic Church was Christ's Church, but I did not agree with Alex turning our church services into a Mass.

His ministers became polarized and began to have heated discussions with him. Alex had changed from having the communion service once a month to having it every Sunday. Then, when he began to call communion the body and the blood of the Lord, they became so upset they began to leave one by one. Members of the congregation began responding the same way when we had communion. I saw friends who had been with us for nearly forty years get up and walk out. But there were those who stayed and believed, and even though Alex didn't have holy orders, I believe God honored our faith and the respect we had for his table. We obeyed the Scripture we were taught, 1 Corinthians 11:27–30, concerning the Lord's table. If any man drank or ate unworthily, he would be guilty of sinning against the body and blood of the Lord. We were celebrating communion one Sunday when the Lord gave me new insight about his table. He revealed to me that some of his people really didn't understand what his table was all about. As he conveyed this message to me, his presence seemed to embody the sacramental table. He made it clear that his table was nothing to play with, that it is dangerous to eat at the Lord's table if you know you are not right with the Lord. Many of his children, he revealed, are not aware of the danger they are in. Like children playing around a hot, potbellied stove, if they get too close they will get burned.

Alex continued to choreograph the services as the apostles had done them in the early Church. He would preach like a Pentecostal preacher, and he would emulate the apostolic tradition during the rest of the service. We were doing all the kneeling, standing, sitting, and it seemed like aerobics to us. Alex also instituted a processional every Sunday, and I questioned that too. It all seemed very foreign, so I wondered why on earth we had to go through all these aerobics and processionals. The Holy Spirit answered me by speaking to my heart: *When a diplomat goes to another country, the red carpet is rolled out for him, and the honor guard is present. But here you are ushering in the King of Kings, Ruler over all the kings of the earth and in heaven. When the leaders of the Church are coming in carrying the cross, they are ushering in the Spirit of the living God.*

I began to understand why processing in with the cross reminds us of what Jesus has done for us. We are there to show our love and appreciation for all that he has done. We are there to be filled with his love by being in his presence. We are to be so filled that it spills over into our homes, businesses, schools, and neighborhoods. As David says in the twenty-third Psalm, "My cup runneth over." When we kneel to say prayers, we are giving respect out of reverence for the King of Kings and Lord of Lords. We certainly wouldn't want to give haphazard respect for the Lord.

Some of these things were beginning to make sense, but there was so much more I was trying to make sense of.

5

Mother Mary

I was the loudest voice against Mary. Why should I pray to Mary? I could go directly to Jesus. Why did Catholics make such a big deal over her? Why did they place such significance on her being Queen Mother? I certainly had not studied that in Scripture! Of course my husband, as pastor, did talk about Mary at Christmastime and Easter—about all she went through at the foot of her Son's Cross. So I had a curiosity about her, but I would stay up until three in the morning arguing with Alex about Mary.

I didn't know in what perspective to place Mary—what role she would play in my personal life. I knew she was the mother of Jesus. I believed she helped raise other children, but I couldn't relate to Mary. I felt like the child of a single parent. I was raised only with loving Jesus and talking only to *him*. He was more than my big brother, more than my friend. He was my Savior; he was my Lord; he was my King. He was the very essence of my survival. I felt it was by Providence that I was placed in a Christian home when my biological home fell apart. It was my Lord who provided for us later when my foster father left my foster mother. There were many experiences throughout my life that taught me to trust Jesus and lean on him for everything. So I felt like the child of a single parent because I could only relate to Jesus, not to his mother, Mary.

I accepted the fact that Mary was the mother of Jesus. But when we started attending some Catholic Masses, I would see the statues of Mary with a crown on her head, and I would think, "There is a little idol worship going on here!"

After Dennis Walters started coming over every Tuesday to provide catechesis for us, I told him I couldn't find much about Mary, and I needed to have substantiation through the Scriptures. He helped me find the many places in the Bible that powerfully describe Mary, and the Lord opened my eyes to understand the beautiful and amazing role Mary plays in the life of the Church. She said Yes to the will of God and ushered in a new dispensation—the age of grace. God does use the weak to confound the wise.

There were some major points of contention I needed to deal with. As Pentecostals, whenever we read Luke 8:19–21 or Mark 3:31–35, we thought Jesus was disrespecting his mother. "There came then his brethren and his mother, and, standing without, sent unto him, calling him. And the multitude sat about him, and they said unto him, Behold, thy mother and thy brethren without seek for thee. And he answered them, saying, 'Who is my mother, or my brethren?' And he looked round about on them which sat about him, and said, 'Behold my mother and my brethren! For whosoever shall do the will of God, is my brother and sister and mother'" (Mk 3:31–35).

The Lord opened my mind when he helped me to understand that he was paying tremendous respect to his mother because she *always* did the will of God, highlighted most vividly at the Incarnation and the crucifixion. Mary said Yes to God, then gave her Son away to the work of God. She is truly the Mother of the Church by participating with God in allowing Jesus to suffer and die on the Cross, bringing deliverance to all of mankind. If anyone is to be honored, it is to be Mary. Who did the will of God more perfectly than Mary? We can do God's will when the going is easy. But it is much more difficult under pressure and turmoil. And I don't know who was under more pressure and turmoil than Mother Mary. She was tempted like Jesus, but she chose not to give in. She was completely without sin.

As Protestants, we sometimes took issue with Mary's holiness. The Lord helped me to understand just how incredibly holy Mary was. If Moses was told to take off his shoes because God's presence made the place where he was walking holy ground, wouldn't the vessel God put himself into be that much more holy? God put himself into Mary as the tabernacle of the Lord. We only need to use some common sense when we are reading Scripture. Moses had to take his shoes off, and God only spoke with him for a few minutes. God dwelled inside Mary for nine months. It doesn't take a rocket scientist to figure out just how holy Mary truly must be. She is called holy because she chose to live holiness and did so by the grace of God. She said Yes to God, and she meant it. God had prepared her as a special vessel, and he filled her full of grace. "Wherefore when he cometh into the world, he saith, Sacrifice and offering thou wouldest not, but a body hast thou prepared me" (Heb 10:5).

And, of course, we too are to revere Mary just as Christ did. "And Mary said, My soul doth magnify the Lord, And my spirit hath rejoiced in God my Saviour. For he hath regarded the low estate of his handmaiden: for, behold, from henceforth all generations shall call me blessed. For he that is mighty hath done to me great things; and holy is his name" (Lk 1:46-49).

Then there was the fact that the Church called Mary a perpetual virgin. This didn't ring true with me because I had read in Scripture that Jesus had brothers, and I wondered

how Mary could be called a perpetual virgin when obvi-
ously she had other children. I didn't understand that there
was no word in the Aramaic language (the language of Jesus'
time) for cousins and other relatives, so all were called brothers and sisters. Well, this point led to a midnight arguing
session with my husband.

This is part of the problem with *Sola Scriptura*—taking
the *Bible alone* as one's authority. The tradition of the Church
and Church history play a huge part in understanding the
Scriptures, but most of us don't bother to look into the
meaning of the words at the time of Jesus or find out what
the history and customs were two thousand years ago. Some
of our customs and traditions and the language we use in
America today are totally unacceptable or can even be insult-
ing in other countries. Before going to another country we
would be wise to study their language, customs, and traditions. If this is true today, why do we think we can read
and understand the Bible when we haven't studied the language, customs, and traditions of the Jews two thousand
years ago?

Then when I read again 2 Thessalonians 2:15, "Therefore, brethren, stand fast, and hold the traditions which ye
have been taught, whether by word, or our epistle", my
eyes were opened to the error of *Sola Scriptura*. There it
was—right in the Bible itself—that the Bible was *not* the
only source! It just exploded in my mind! That one verse
of Scripture opened an entire new avenue and took the
restrictions off many things as far as Mary was concerned.
The Lord just took the blinders off, and the scales fell from
my eyes.

This allowed me to look into Jewish tradition. In Jewish
tradition, it was the children's responsibility to care for the
parents. In John 19:25–27, it says: "Now there stood by the

cross of Jesus his mother, and his mother's sister, Mary the
wife of Cleophas, and Mary Magdalene. When Jesus therefore saw his mother, and the disciple standing by, whom he
loved, he saith unto his mother, Woman, behold thy son!
Then saith he to the disciple, Behold thy mother! And from
that hour that disciple took her unto his own home."

That passage does not say that John was a brother or
even a relative, but rather a disciple. Now if the Law of
Moses said the children must take care of the parents, then
why would Jesus give his mother to a disciple if she had
other children? Jesus would not break the law. He said,
"Think not that I am come to destroy the law, or the prophets: I am not come to destroy, but to fulfill" (Mt 5:17). All
of this went through my mind as the Lord released me from
Sola Scriptura.

One night, as Alex and I were sitting at the dinner table,
I began asking him more questions about Mary. We had
recently attended a Catholic conference at Franciscan University in Steubenville, Ohio, and I wondered about the
statues of Mary wearing a crown I had seen there and in
other Catholic churches. Alex explained how in Jewish cus-
tom the mother always sat on the throne with her son the
king because the king had so many wives. It was expected
that the mother would take her rightful place alongside her
son, and so it should be with Mary. That made sense to
me, but I wanted to know how I could relate to Mother
Mary on a daily basis. He reminded me of our wise, older
"church mother" at Zion Congregational Church. Those
seeking advice and intercessory prayer would go to this holy
woman and ask her as a confidante to pray for them. Alex
pointed out that Mary was the Catholic Church Mother.
She was the one who guided the disciples in the Upper
Room. How else would they know to wait for the guidance

of the Holy Spirit? Mary was the only one who intimately knew the Holy Spirit. Mary was the only one who had been overshadowed by the Holy Spirit. She carried Jesus in her womb for nine months. She symbolized the Ark of the Covenant. She was there on the day of Pentecost.

Who else could be such a perfect Church Mother as Mary?

Still, I wondered how Mary, the Mother of Jesus, who sits on the throne with her Son, could relate to my everyday problems and appreciate my cries for help. I came to understand that she was fully human too. She too went through the trials of dealing with a husband (it never says anywhere in the Bible that Joseph was without sin), neighbors, family members, and running a household. Like Jesus, there were times when she was tempted to sin, but we know that she was full of grace and made the choice never to give in to sin. So she is able to relate to us on a most personal level and to intercede for us because she truly understands our daily trials and temptations.

Then, as I reread the Scriptures, I realized that Mary, in her meekness, humility, and silence, was speaking volumes by her actions, not with her words, and not just to the women of the time, but to all of us today. The Lord was letting me know that she was the epitome of meekness and humility. She trusted in the will of God even through her incredible suffering. Mary accepted God's will even unto allowing her Son, who had done nothing wrong, to be crucified on the Cross. When that sword was piercing her heart, she didn't say a word. She stood back with a meek and quiet spirit. She was saying, "Lord, I'm letting your will be done." God was working in her a greater virtue because of her willingness to say Yes to his will. It has produced a testimony for all time.

God prepared her to endure this Cross. He filled her full of grace. The Lord was preparing me and letting me know that Mary was, indeed, full of grace, and that we too are to call her blessed. We cannot go through difficult situations that are handed to us unless we ask God for grace. And we can ask Mother Mary to pray with us for that grace. How much more, when Mother Mary prays for us, will God give us the desires of our hearts? We don't go to people on earth and ask them to pray for us because they have nice clothes or a fine house. We go to those who, like our church mothers, show the working of grace in their lives and their closeness to God. Who was closer to God than Mary? Who was more full of grace than Mother Mary, the first tabernacle of the Word Incarnate?

Women of today often don't understand that true freedom comes from being submissive to God. We are perfected through our trials. God is working in us a far greater glory. He is leading us toward perfection. God *will* give us victory; it just may not be the way we think it should be.

There were many times I wanted to say I know this is the Church that Christ left on earth, but why do we have to close up our church and go into the Catholic Church? Why can't we have our own special parish? My husband submitted to what he was told to do, but I was still questioning. The Lord told me not to get in the way. He let me know that Alex was under enough pressure. I felt like Sarah following her husband into unknown territory. It was as though God were saying to me, "Just follow me here." Later I understood Mary as the perfect example of submitting to the will of God, and I tried to do my best to emulate her.

People would ask how we could leave our church, friends, and family as we did. I would answer, "How could Mother

Mary endure all she did and give up so very much? It was
because of grace."

The Lord allowed me to see that if we look in the Bible
we have Mother Mary as a perfect example. The Lord exalted
her. He allowed me to see that she truly was the Queen
Mother of the Church. In Revelation, just as in Jewish cus-
tom, she was the one who was crowned. She was assumed
into heaven to sit on the throne with her Son.

As I learned to pray the Rosary, at first I couldn't understand why I felt such great peace. Then I began to realize
that when you are in the presence of people who have given
their lives totally over to God, they exhibit great peace. I
believe because Mary gave herself over so completely to
God to be used totally for his will that she was filled with
God's peace even unto the moment of his death. Now, as I
pray the Rosary, I believe the peace I feel is due to the
presence of Mother Mary.

Who else could be such a perfect Mother as Mary? Our
church mothers were very helpful to us, but Mother
Mary is, without question, the best Church Mother I've
ever known.

6

Paradigm Shift

All the while the Lord was dealing with me and opening my understanding of the Catholic Church through Scriptures and theological teachings about Mary, the saints, and oral tradition, life was still going on. There were times I just wanted everything to stop so I could digest all the information I was being inundated with. But I was still a mother, a grandmother, an employee (I had gone back to work when funds dwindled as members left the congregation), and a college student. I was still the pastor's wife in the evenings and weekends, taking care of my husband's appointments. It was not as if I could go on retreat to think about things. I never knew who would be stopping over at the house, so I had to make sure everything was always clean. Life was crazy!

It seemed as though the days I was having my greatest struggles would be the days one of my sons would call and ask me to babysit. I would say, "Lord, can't you wait until I can figure this all out?" I wanted to push the pause button. But life continued.

We still had the expenses of the church too—$1,600 for gas or air conditioning, plus all the other bills each month. People and their wallets and purses were walking out of the door, but the expenses remained constant. As our monetary base shrunk, we had to borrow from other areas. We really had to rob Peter to pay Paul.

I longed for some kind of support system among family and friends, but none existed. My kids were searching and hurting as I was. My daughters-in-law were asking questions. The women at the church were asking questions. It seemed that everything was hurled at me at once. Even my husband couldn't give the support I needed. He was battling his own demons, and I could hear him walking the floors at two o'clock in the morning. He too was busy studying and finding answers for the many questions our church members had. They would call at all hours.

And it wasn't as though our people had friends or relatives they could call for information about the Catholic Church. Most of us came from a long line of Protestant or Pentecostal teaching. We knew no one who had gone down the path we were traveling. And, of course, we had been told not to go outside the Bible (*Sola Scriptura*), or we would get off track spiritually—something we guarded against.

My twin sister, Dianne, and I were never really close, and she said she wouldn't even talk to me about this. Debbie is my friend as well as my sister, but she couldn't comprehend all that was going on. Still, she would always tell me, "Donna, support your husband." Many of my sisters in the Lord totally dropped me like a hot potato. They couldn't grasp the fact that the Catholic Church is Christ's Church. Alex was completely exhausted, and the church was in upheaval. I felt totally isolated.

The one bright spot was the love that the parishioners at Christ the King Catholic Church in Ann Arbor showered upon us. In spite of their busy schedules, Steve Ray and his family and Dennis Walters and his family visited us whenever they could. They provided a wonderful support system when it was most needed.

But I had no one really to talk to on a daily basis about Catholicism, and I literally walked my apartment floor asking God to send me someone. I believe, however, in that initial period, that the Lord wanted me to pick up the King James Version of the Bible. He used it to teach me what I needed to know about Mary, praying to the saints, Purgatory, oral tradition, and the Magisterium. I read additional books on these topics as well.

The people of Christ the King would bring over boxes of books for us and leave them at our door. Conversion stories were very helpful. The conversion stories in *Surprised by Truth*, edited by Patrick Madrid, were like a support system for me. It was as though these people were coming in and putting structure under the knowledge I had. I felt that I was getting new beams under my thought pattern to strengthen the knowledge I already had and to remove the errors I had been told about Catholicism.

God never puts more on you than you can bear. But I knew I was in a real battle. I felt the Lord really wanted me to come to him in prayer. I felt compelled to pray. So when I went to work, I would first go into the bathroom and pray. I knew I couldn't get through the day without that time of prayer.

We, of course, were not the only ones suffering. The people who came with us into the Catholic Church had to leave their friends and families behind too. Family members turned against them. They were battling just as hard as we were. They followed us because they too had discovered the truth. My husband had told them to research it for themselves. He would explain, "If I tell you Chicago is on the map, don't get angry with me because you don't believe that to be true. Go and look for yourself. By the same token, don't get mad if I tell you the Catholic Church is the Church of Jesus Christ. I'm just the messenger. Go and find out for yourself."

That same message applied to our children. When our sons and their wives began questioning what direction their father and I were heading in, we had a family dinner. When we told them we were becoming Catholic, it didn't end very well. Alex told them they shouldn't follow us blindly, but to do some research for themselves. Benjamin was quite vocal and wanted to know why we would give up twenty-five years of ministry and go into a church that "doesn't like Blacks".

The Lord helped me realize that the love of Janet and Steve Ray and other Catholics helped draw me into the Church and that that kind of love was what I needed to show my children. The Lord told me not to push Catholicism down their throats, but to pray that their eyes would be opened. God revealed to me that a mother's love is what they needed. He said to pray for an opportunity to share information about Catholicism that would be beneficial to them. Prayer and showing them the kind of love we had received was instrumental in drawing them into the Church.

Our children did not come into the Church because we came in, but because they discovered the truth for themselves. Others also came into the Church because they based their decision on truth, and they are still in the Catholic Church. We all were in constant prayer in our quest for the truth. Prayer was essential to bringing us through this paradigm shift.

One thing we all found out: when God changes your paradigm, he doesn't always do it in a comfortable setting. Sometimes God allows pressure to help in the making of you. God takes the pressure of the situation to help you emerge like a diamond. You need to be ready to go with

God wherever he takes you, even though it may take you out of your comfort zone.

God certainly took us out of our comfort zone. As Alex read the *Catechism of the Catholic Church*, he realized that to discover truth and not to follow through with it would be a sin. He knew he had to enter the Catholic Church. We had originally hoped to remain in our church as an African-American, charismatic, Catholic parish, but that was not to be. We were told by the archdiocese that we could not do that. I don't think the archdiocese believed we understood the magnitude of what we were doing, but we did. There are so many monks and cloistered nuns devoted to prayer, praying that Protestants and Catholics become one. Those prayers are being answered. Miracles are happening. We were one of those miracles—part of that answered prayer! But we obeyed the directives of the Detroit Archdiocese and ended up selling our beautiful Maranatha building. We were instructed by the archdiocese to enter the RCIA (Rite of Christian Initiation of Adults) program at Saint Suzanne Parish in Detroit.

The day of the Rite of Acceptance at Saint Suzanne's, there was a torrential downpour. On the way to the church, Alex said he didn't think very many from Maranatha would show up. When we arrived, our hearts were so warmed because all sixty-two of us (including Alex and me) who had said they wanted to become Catholic were there. (Fifty-four of us eventually did enter the Church.) The Lord encouraged our hearts. We all marched down the walkway and stood in the vestibule of the church. Alex was given a wooden block and a hammer, and as he pounded on the door, the echo reverberated in the church. The door was opened, and we marched to the altar. There Alex handed his robes to Saint Suzanne's pastor, Father Dennis Duggan, and said, "Whatever the Church wants me to do, I will do." Then Alex got on his knees and asked Father Dennis to bless him. It was incredibly touching for me.

The following Sunday, the reality of the situation set in. I give a lot of credit to Father Dennis. He tried his best to be the liaison between us and the community, to bring his parishioners and the folks from Maranatha successfully together, but they were simply unprepared for us.

Saint Suzanne's was a primarily Caucasian, older parish. They had been that way for decades. One Sunday they were as they had always been, and the next, there were sixty-two African-American Pentecostals in their church saying, "Hello! Here we are to stay!" While we were blessed with a number of parishioners who welcomed us and reached out to us with the love of Christ, many were simply not ready to accept us, and it showed in their greeting and body language that they really didn't want us there. Many had preconceived notions that we were a bunch of out-of-control, screaming Pentecostals that were invading their world. They didn't have a clue how to minister to us and didn't want to try. They were like deer in headlights. They were stunned and didn't know how to take us. Some didn't want to worship with us because we were Black. They changed Masses so they wouldn't have to go to church with us. And this was Christ's Church? Alex had taught us that Christ's Church accepted everyone. Our first impression was "not so!"

I understood why some of the people of Saint Suzanne's felt betrayed and confused by our presence, but it didn't stop the hurt. We were all hurt. We had given up everything, and it wasn't like we could go back. We no longer had a church! We had just come out of the fire from our own church and the Protestant community, where we had suffered the painful rejection of our loved ones because we were coming into the Catholic Church. Friends and family had already rejected us. Then we came into this painful rejection at Saint Suzanne's because of our color and because of preconceived notions about who we were. It was like adding insult to injury.

But there were some, both Caucasian and African-American, who did reach out to us and welcome us with love. If it were not for those few and for Father Dennis, our experience at Saint Suzanne's would have been nearly unbearable.

Later I realized that I would have hurt less had I focused more on the future and what God wanted me to do. But many times (and I too was guilty of this) we get caught up in the emotions of the moment. The devil was working on me. There was a myriad of feelings racing through my mind. I had been in ministry for twenty-five years, and now I was in a place where I had no voice and no say, and I didn't feel wanted either. I struggled with so many thoughts, but the thing that kept me at Saint Suzanne's was my ability to relate to the suffering of Mother Mary. I knew that Christ wanted me in his Church, and I said Yes to that.

I could relate to Mother Mary. I could understand some of the pain she felt. She did God's will in spite of the hurt. I could relate to suffering and loss. Even though we were in God's will, it didn't stop us from feeling abandoned or alone. It didn't stop the pain. It didn't stop the hurt.

To do God's will we had to leave our ministry, family, and friends to come into a place where many didn't want us or understand why we were there. Sometimes Alex would talk with me all the way home. He would say, "Donna, don't focus on the few. Remember all the loving people in Christ's Church."

And there were many. Parishioners at Christ the King emailed other Catholic churches and informed them of our situation. People at those churches emailed us with support and to tell us they were praying for us. Only God knows how very much we appreciated those prayers. These dear ones truly showed us the love of the Catholic Church.

And we were sustained by the knowledge that God had a plan for us.

7

God's Plan

In spite of all the difficulties we were going through, the "Maranatha group"—as we were called at Saint Suzanne's— knew that God's plan for us was to become members of his Church. And, no matter what, that was precisely what we were determined to do. I had already made up my mind that if I couldn't come in through the door, I would find a window.

That first Sunday, however, I felt at loose ends—like I was out of place, disjointed. Pastors' wives are to be their husband's eyes and ears—to work behind the scenes and aid them, making sure things run smoothly. We train ourselves to see whatever goes wrong and to let our husbands know so they can do whatever is necessary to help their people—visitor or member—receive all that God intended for them to gain while worshipping at or visiting our church.

Now I was in a new situation, a new church where I had no input whatsoever. I felt helpless—like a fish out of water. I began seeing things that needed to be changed. I went into pastor's wife mode, and I had to catch myself. Wait a minute—this is not my place! I was completely lost. Not only that, but I felt beat up and scarred inside. I felt wounded. I felt like we had been through a war just to get into the Catholic Church. The community we had come from, for the most part, didn't understand why we left, and the people there were feeling betrayed and hostile. They

rejected us, and here we were in a new church that didn't
seem too thrilled with us either.

Of course, our trials were just beginning. The Sunday
after the Rite of Acceptance, we were scheduled to begin
RCIA, and Saint Suzanne's had gathered a team of teachers
to instruct us in the Catholic faith. But most of them were
not prepared for us.

One Sunday, Mary—a very good teacher, who came out
from Christ the King—would teach from the *Catechism of
the Catholic Church*. The next week we had a laicized priest
who was teaching with a detectible degree of animosity.
He spoke about the Eucharist being dry and sticking to the
roof of your mouth. He was on the verge of being irrev-
erent. Then we had a third-grade teacher who wanted to
"introduce" God to us—this to a group of adults who already
had established a very deep and reverent relationship with
God, a relationship that put God at the very center of their
lives. We had people from Saint Suzanne assigned to us as
mentors. One of our people asked a question about Purgatory, and her mentor tapped her on the shoulder and said,
"We really don't believe in Purgatory anymore."

If Alex had not taught us all he had about Catholicism
before coming to Saint Suzanne's, we would have been totally
confused and discouraged. He knew more about the Catholic Church than many Catholics did and had been teaching us for some time. He had made Catholicism amazingly
clear by explaining at length and in great detail such things
as Mary, the saints, the Magisterium, Purgatory, the sacraments, and oral tradition. Alex, because of his abilities and
knowledge, was asked by Mary, our RCIA leader, to help
with the instructions. He began teaching the Maranatha
group by the fourth or fifth Sunday into our RCIA experience, alternating weeks with Mary.

About this time we became concerned that the children might not be getting the kind of catechesis they needed either. I had heard complaints from some of the parents concerning the children's RCIA program. The children were reporting their dissatisfaction to their parents, so I spoke with the director of religious education on several occasions regarding the parents' concerns, but to no avail. It was painfully obvious that they were not prepared for our children either. Looking back on the experience now, I believe the biggest problem was that lack of preparedness. Our entire situation was so incredibly unique, and there was certainly no model for bringing an African-American Pentecostal congregation into a predominantly white, older, established Catholic parish.

Some days it was a battle. We came out of such a fervent, fiery worship into this faith where there seemed to be such apathy—yet this was the Church that was left by Jesus Christ. There were days when I would say, "I'm not going back to Saint Suzanne's. I'm not going to enter the Catholic Church." But I would always come back to the fact that this was Christ's Church. I knew that God's plan for me was to be a member of his Church, and I had come too far, come through too much to turn back. Thankfully, there were a number of people from Saint Suzanne's who tried very hard to make things work—especially Father Dennis Duggan.

The night of the Easter Vigil, April 14, 2001, was the pinnacle of that year for me. I had never attended or witnessed an Easter Vigil before and wasn't sure what to expect. After lighting our candles from the new Paschal candle, we followed it, processing into the darkness of the sanctuary, beautifully lighting the church as we moved toward the altar. I began to think about Christ's death, and I went through the steps of the crucifixion, death, and burial. Going through this visual process really etched those events in my mind. When the lights were turned on, it was another visual expression of the light that Christ brought to the earth. In days of old, God would reveal himself through the prophets, but through Christ's death and resurrection, he has opened the door of salvation for everyone to know him as Lord and Savior, and he has revealed the precious jewel of his Church.

As we approached the altar, we came to stand in front of Father Dennis. He was so excited. Our sponsors stood behind us. Dennis Walters was Alex' sponsor, and my dear friend Janet Ray was mine. Alex was like a Moses to me. He had led his people, and we had finally reached our destination. I could hear the relief in his voice when he said, "I'm finally home." I felt exactly the same way. It had been a very long journey, but we were finally home. Alex received his First Communion on his knees, and I did the same.

By the night of that Easter Vigil, I knew Alex had done exactly what the Lord had called upon him to do—he had followed God's mind and led us all according to the plan God had for us. In 1 Corinthians 11:1 it says: "Be ye followers of me, even as I also am of Christ." I had always tried to follow my husband as my pastor, but as he drew closer to apostolic teaching and consequently to the Catholic Church, I felt he had turned a corner on us. Later I realized that he was correct in turning that corner. As a servant of Christ, it was his responsibility to follow the mind of God, not his own mind.

I would not have had the courage to follow my husband into the Church had I not seen this man live a holy life. The Bible says: "And we beseech you, brethren, to know them which labour among you, and are over you in the Lord, and admonish you; And to esteem them very highly in love for their work's sake. And be at peace among yourselves" (1 Thess 5:12–13). As long as we know those that labor among us, those who fast and pray as they seek God, we have the responsibility to pray for the wisdom to follow them, even when new things are revealed. The Bible also teaches us to honor them. "Let the elders that rule well be counted worthy of double honour, especially they who labour in the word and doctrine" (1 Tim 5:17).

Alex was right on track. God leads us in ways that we may not always understand. Many times God has guided his people in operating "outside the box". I am a witness that God will unveil his plan if you are willing to follow the leader he has put in charge of accomplishing the task. Sometimes if I read the Scriptures and still didn't understand, I would kneel by my bed and pray, asking God to reveal the jewels that he was directing Alex to give us. Eventually, that's exactly what he did! As I searched the Scriptures, I found the answers I sought. They were in there, in the King James Version of the Bible, just as plain as could be.

There were so many at Maranatha who openly fought what Alex was trying to teach. They didn't understand, and they got up and left. I recognized that they were not disrespecting my husband, the man; they were failing to comprehend the Spirit of God in the man.

Our constant challenge is to say Yes to the direction God wants us to go. That is especially true for the leaders in Christ's Church—the Catholic Church. There are leaders in other denominations, not in Christ's Church yet, that do what God tells them to do. Even without knowing the full truth, they are being directed by God (Rom 2:14–26).

We, as Pentecostals, didn't have the fullness of truth, but we followed as much as we knew, and God counted that for righteousness. God was leading my husband for twenty-five years, and for most of those twenty-five years, we knew next to nothing about the Catholic Church. But we honestly desired to follow God with all our hearts, and he led us to the fullness of the truth. God had to get us to the point where we could receive this precious jewel of knowledge he was preparing to give to us. Still, some were not ready because they were looking at the man, my husband, their pastor, instead of at Christ working through the man.

We who are in Christ's Church must be patient with our brothers and sisters yet to come in. Jesus prayed that we would all be one (Jn 17:11). For a thousand years that is exactly what we were, although some heresies arose that had to be corrected. The Catholic Church was and is the Church of Jesus Christ. We will again be one and God allows all of us to be the instruments to bring that about.

On October 1, 2005, Alex and I were blessed as he was ordained a permanent deacon by Cardinal Adam Maida for the Detroit Archdiocese. I have witnessed firsthand Alex' frustrations and battles as he sought the truth and found it in the Church. Now I can look back with joy upon his discovery of the fullness of the faith in the Church that Christ left and his desire to not only come into the Church, but to be a servant of God within the Church.

I was moved by the sacredness of the ordination service and by seeing the Magisterium in action—appointing deacons to serve the Church through their special gifts. I witnessed a vibrant Church in action—a Church that is alive and well, growing and thriving. I felt such awe and a more pronounced respect for the structure God left in his Church. Even after two thousand years, the majesty of God's Church has not waned.

Because Alex and I yielded by saying Yes to Christ's Church, God has blessed us in making us witnesses all across the nation. He has allowed us to share our testimony of what he, in his great mercy, has done for us. And he is opening the doors of other nations to our giving our testimony and being servants of his grace and power. God is opening the eyes of his servants not yet in his Church and is bringing them to the Church.

I thank God that he has allowed Alex and me to be a part of this miracle of grace.

8

Our Church

I picture myself walking through the wilderness of this earth. God is in heaven, but he has not abandoned us. He has placed his Church on this earth to give us all the help we need in order to one day join him in heaven. Hallelujah! When I battle through all the trials I encounter during the week, I know I can come into this Church and can give praise for all he has done for me. I can gain strength and inspiration from Mother Mary and the saints, who were victors even before they went to heaven. I can receive the Word of God through the priest, and I can be filled with inspiration. I can gain inspiration through my brothers and sisters, who build me up through their charisms. That gives me the strength to go out and spread the Good News of the Gospel. We are a spiritual community, and these gifts shouldn't just stay in the church building. We take these charisms—what we have received—out into the community to serve as helpers to one another.

Our strength is derived from the Eucharist—the bread of the Lord's table. Every time I take Communion, I am awed by how the Lord humbles himself to be my food. I can take him into myself, and he is my food. He is our physical and spiritual Manna. "God is our refuge and strength, a very present help in trouble" (Ps 46:1). Eating his body and drinking his blood is our strength. That is our present help.

When we receive the Eucharist, it is not just for ourselves alone, but to give to our brothers through our actions.

We are servants of Christ. By nature we are selfish, but the more we are filled with the love of Christ, the more we will desire to be loving and giving persons. Our minds will be centered on heavenly things. When you are revived, you are concerned with what God is concerned about, and he is concerned about lifting souls out of bondage.

Our Catholic Church is the filling station of life, and we are to have life abundantly! It also equips us with the armor we need to go out into the world—into Satan's territory—and take back our homes and neighborhoods. It is a battle, and we are to be salt wherever God asks us to go.

I now understand that the Catholic Church was the structure Jesus left for us. He didn't hand us a Bible, he left us the Church. When we witness to people about Christianity, we don't just hand them a Bible and say, "God bless you! So long!" We want to give them structure, and we have the good sense to bring them to our church, to a body of believers and a pastor. Do we think, then, that God *didn't* have enough sense to leave the structure of the Church for us? Christ left us the structure of the Catholic Church—a Church that the gates of hell would never prevail against. She has the same basic structure today that she had two thousand years ago. The content of the Christian Bible wasn't determined until nearly four hundred years later, and it was determined by a Council of bishops of—guess what—the Catholic Church!

It makes sense. It is all so logical.

The Catholic Church is in every country, with every color and every nationality. The Spirit will enlighten and lead the faithful into all truth. Those that really want to know the truth must educate themselves concerning the Catholic Church. Many of the things we were taught as Pentecostals about the Catholic Church were erroneous. When I learned

the truth about the Catholic Church, I didn't cease being
Pentecostal; I simply became a fulfilled Pentecostal. Of course,
the process was not easy. It caused the breakup of families.
It put mothers against daughters, sisters against sisters, and
fathers against sons. That doesn't mean that it wasn't the
will of God for us to come into the Church. Jesus told us
this would happen (Mt 10:34–39).

To others who are thinking about coming into the Church
I would say: Don't be afraid of where God wants you to go.
God will reveal where he wants you to go as long as you
follow his plan. You may feel lost, hurt, and discouraged,
but don't forget, our Lord suffered as he hung on the Cross.
He was doing God's will.

God has a plan that is beyond our understanding, and we
need to follow him even though we may lose everything. I
eventually came to the point where I understood that. I
could relate to Job. Naked I came into this world; naked
I am leaving. Lord, not my will, but yours be done. I had
no idea what was in store for me. I had to give up twenty-
five years of working with my husband as a pastor's wife. I
had to give up my ministry as well as some of my family
and friends. But you can never outdo God's generosity. When
you put your total trust in God, even when you feel like
you can't make it any further, God will never let you go
under. He will send someone to strengthen you. He will
send people you would never expect to encourage you. He
will strengthen you through the Church, the priest, a homily, his Word, or a song. Some days I would be struggling,
and someone would come up and give me a hug or just a
smile. Those people didn't know how much they were ministering to me.

As a Catholic, I have also had the opportunity to be a
minister to others. About the time we were beginning our

journey into the Church, the priest sex scandals began sur-
facing. We were celebrating our first anniversary as Catholics when Father Dennis Duggan was removed from Saint
Suzanne's (his case remains unresolved at this time). Some
of the parishioners found out when they heard about it on
the evening news and were very upset. It was like a funeral.
I was on the parish council then and was able to help some
of them through this. They looked to us, the Maranatha
group, and realized we had already suffered similar pain with
the loss of our church.

There was a great deal of questioning and doubt within
the Church at that time, but I never once doubted God's
plan in all this. The Holy Spirit helped me to understand
that this God who spoke the earth and the heavens into
existence is certainly capable of correcting whatever is wrong
in his Church. It is Satan's tactics that bring about hope-
lessness. But Christ's truth brings hope. He shows what is
wrong and corrects through prayer.

I believe God is bringing his Church back to its first
glory in the days after Pentecost. God will take down those
that continue to do evil in his Church. He will raise up
priests and leaders after his own Heart. He will use them to
bring about knowledge of the power and glory of his Church.
The Lord is opening up the doors because he wants to revive
his Church. We have not yet seen what the Church will be
like in those days. God is gathering everyone with one mind
and one goal to be the voice and power of his Church on
earth. There is coming a time when God's Church will be
totally awesome in the earth, and nothing, nothing will be
able to stand against her.

We must not complain about our leaders, but pray for
them. We can't give up if things don't happen immediately.
We must be persistent in prayer. We are in the greatest

Church on earth—Christ's Church. The gates of hell will *never* prevail against the Church, and the Spirit of Christ will be with us *always!*

Now that I am in Christ's Church, I feel as if a table has been spread before me with all the delicious delicacies too numerous to taste. I am experiencing the "unsearchable riches of Christ" (Eph 3:8). Meditating on all the incredible goodness God has bestowed on us, this is my prayer: *Lord, thank you for leading Alex and me to your Church. Give us the strength and the will and the mind to be totally immersed in you and your will. Give us the strength to stand in the hard times and the love to overlook whatever faults its members may have. In Jesus name, amen.*

Photo 31. Donna delivers the second reading during the diaconate ordination Mass of her husband.

Photo 32. Cardinal Adam Maida accepts the promise of
obedience from diaconate candidate Alex Jones.

Photo 33. The diaconate candidates (Alex is second from
  left) lay prostrate before the altar during the
  Litany of the Saints.

252

Photo 34. Cardinal Adam Maida confers diaconal ordination on candidate Alex Jones through the laying
on of hands.

Photo 35. Father Robert McCabe (left) and Deacon Patrick
Conlen assist Alex as he is vested as a deacon.
Father McCabe is pastor of Saint Mary of Redford and Saint Suzanne/Our Lady Gate of Heaven
and administrator of St. Thomas Aquinas parishes, all in Detroit where Alex is now serving
as deacon. Deacon Patrick Conlen serves at Saint
John Neumann Church in Canton, Michigan,
where Alex was a deacon intern.

Photo 36. Cardinal Maida places the Book of Gospels into Alex' hands as he says, "Receive the Gospel of Christ, whose herald you have become. Believe what you read; teach what you believe; and practice what you teach."

Photo 37. The Jones' sons Marc (left) and Joseph assist in the Presentation of Gifts.

Photo 38. The newly ordained Deacon Jones serving during the Mass of Ordination.

Photo 39. Following the Mass of Ordination, retired Auxiliary Bishop Moses Anderson, SSE (left); Deacon
Michael Somervell; Deacon Jene Baughman; Cardinal Adam Maida; Deacon Michael Chesley;
Deacon Alex Jones; Auxiliary Bishop John
Quinn; and Monsignor John Zenz pose in front
of the cathedral rectory.

Photo 40. Deacon Alex and Donna Jones.

258

Photo 41. Deacon Alex with Father George Williams, pastor of Saint John Neumann Church, Canton, Michigan (left), and Deacon Patrick Conlen of Saint John Neumann Church.

Photo 42. Some of the Jones family after the ordination ceremony and reception. Front row: Benjamin holding baby Alex; Donna; Alex with Joseph, Jr.; Joseph, Sr. holding daughter Bethany. Back row: Tamiia, Alexes, Tamila, and Bianca.

PHOTO CREDITS